Sexual Static

Books by
Morton and Marjorie Hansen Shaevitz

Sexual Static
Making It Together as a Two-Career Couple
The Superwoman Syndrome

Sexual Static

How Men Are Confusing
the Women They Love

Dr. Morton H. Shaevitz

"The Last Word"
by Marjorie Hansen Shaevitz

LITTLE, BROWN AND COMPANY
Boston — Toronto

FIRST EDITION

Library of Congress Cataloging-in-Publication Data

Shaevitz, Morton H.
 Sexual static.

 1. Men — United States — Psychology. 2. Women —
United States — Psychology. 3. Interpersonal relations.
I. Title.
HQ1090.3.S49 1987   305.3'1   86-28733
ISBN 0-315-77292-5

RRD VA

*Published simultaneously in Canada
by Little, Brown & Company (Canada) Limited*

PRINTED IN THE UNITED STATES OF AMERICA

To the memory of my father,
Arthur Shaevitz,
a kind and loving man.

Contents

Acknowledgments

Sexual Static actually began in October 1983, when Larry Kirshbaum, then the publisher of Warner Books, asked me to write a chapter about men for my wife's book, *The Superwoman Syndrome*. The enthusiastic response of many readers of that chapter convinced me that a book explaining men to women was needed.

Bill Phillips, my tough and patient editor, saw early on what this book was to become. During the time we worked together he was exuberant, funny, and risk-taking — shattering all my stereotypes about how senior editors from Boston were supposed to behave.

My special thanks to the coterie of experts on women and relationships who gave my early manuscript a thorough scrutiny, Drs. Judy Bardwick, Natasha Josefowitz, and Alice Sargent. Thanks also to other friends and colleagues who made suggestions along the way, Alan Armstrong, Dr. Spencer Johnson, Drs. Emily and Ken Majer, and Dr. Steven and Susan Schutz.

ACKNOWLEDGMENTS

Margaret McBride always goes beyond what is expected of a literary agent, and did so once again.

Carol Hunt assisted in the early stages, and Florence Friedman and then Cynthia Douglass typed and retyped the many revisions with hardly a grimace. Mignon McCarthy was enormously helpful in ensuring that the needs of single women were addressed and also added a final polish to the entire manuscript.

Finally, an immense debt is due my wife and colleague, Marjorie, whose insights about women show up on many pages and who continued to tell me when I was offtrack, in spite of how I responded.

Author's Note

The ideas in this book have come from over twenty years of working with large numbers of people in my practice as a clinical psychologist, from my own research, and from my readings in the social science literature. I have spent thousands of private hours hearing men's feelings about the women in their lives — about dating them, living with them, marrying them, competing with them, having children with them, loving them, leaving them, needing them, losing them.

I have seen men and women alone and I have seen them as partners. I have also spoken to many audiences across the country who have told me their personal stories. Finally, in my own life as a man, I have been no stranger myself to the conundrum of male-female relationships. I have personally dealt with almost every issue I write about here — at times more successfully than others.

To protect the privacy of the people with whom I

have worked, no case study or anecdote in this book refers to any specific individual or couple. When illustrative material is presented, names and occupations as well as identifying details have been added, deleted, or rearranged.

Sexual Static

I

Adam Was a Lonely Guy

Adam was a lonely guy, but he would never let on to anybody, particularly not to to Eve. Men have always, from the beginning, felt lonely and dependent on women. But men certainly were not going to tell them about it. Better to stand strong, to look cool, to stay in deep disguise, the quintessential silent man, or so the thinking usually goes.

This is not the rare man I describe. This is *most* men, the men that most women are having or trying to have relationships with today. Adam is merely the figurative forefather. When it comes to the opposite sex, the American male has had a long history of being the Great Pretender.

The Great Pretender, our late-twentieth-century Adam, is the guy who now finds himself thrust into the storm of the sex-role revolution. He's found himself taking on an even more complex disguise in response. Most men today present a calm public face, even to lovers and partners, that hides their more turbulent

3

feelings about the shake-up in role relations with the other gender.

Women, of course, have been way out in front in all of this. Over the last several decades, much has changed for women. These changes have been explored and applauded exhaustively in the popular media and continue to be. We have learned a great deal about who women are, what they want, where they're going, and how they are or aren't balancing their complicated lives. Far less is known about what's happened to men during this time. Compared with the avalanche of reporting on women, there's not been much on men to speak of, and what exists may be more distortion and exaggeration than fact.

The public image of men today would lead us all to believe that men have changed right alongside women. Feature films and made-for-TV movies showcase the house husband. Men's consciousness-raising groups make the news (in women's magazines or the women's pages of the paper, of course). Surely, untold thousands have swollen the ranks of a men's liberation movement, and thousands more are waiting for the next weekend of self-exploration to begin. That, more or less, is the popular perception.

Nonsense!

The *un*popular reality is decidedly otherwise.

If the truth be known, in spite of all the transformations in the lives of women, the hearts and minds of men have changed very little. House husbands, in fact, are scarce. A relative handful of men have gone to have their consciousness raised (and even fewer ever followed through).

And the vast majority of American men today are confused, angry, stressed, and downright uncertain about the direction in which things are going for them. They are also unhappy about the many apologetic portrayals

4

of men that float about these days. Men tell me they are fed up with images of the wimp, the workaholic, the insensitive guy.

So why the reality gap?

Part of this may be due to men themselves. Men as a group are not very revealing about feelings. But they're talking even less on this particular subject because the contemporary social climate makes it difficult to acknowledge (to women or in mixed company) anything but positive feelings about women and the changes they're promulgating. They say that questioning the "revolution" or expressing negative feelings about it is often met with a barrage of criticism. Men are accused of being reactionary, chauvinistic, Neanderthal.

So, in public men's comments are supportive, but in a bland, vanillalike way. And I might add that these comments are often what gets reported, giving the impression that most men are pleased by everything that's happening.

However, when men are just with one another, when there are no women present, they have a lot of things to say. After a few minutes of discussion, the true feelings emerge. "Pressured," "resentful," and even "exasperated" are the words I hear.

Because weakness is not acceptable to men, what often don't get expressed are other feelings such as "deserted," "isolated," "ignored," "vulnerable," "uncared for," or "upset." Women often have to deal with the consequences of men's anger. However, they almost never hear men expressing these deeper needs.

What is most confusing is that many men (like the men in this book) are *saying* all the "right things" (often with seeming conviction), but inside they are *feeling* very different. And men (and women) usually behave as they feel rather than as they say.

In the actual, day-to-day relations between the sexes,

this benign male deception is only partially successful. Feelings have a way of making themselves known, one way or another. A man may consistently "say" all the "right" things, for instance. But you know the phrase "actions speak louder than words"?

Consider Steve and Laura.

LAURA: Sometimes I can't understand what's happening. Here I am, living with this thirty-one-year-old man who openly professes a deep commitment to women's equality. He tells me how proud he is that I am advancing in my career. He talks about how much my salary helps "our" budget. All his words to me say *go for it, do it, I support you!*

But then there's that unmistakable look on his face when I tell him I have to work on the weekend or that I'm meeting a friend for lunch. And, in spite of all that I'm doing, he still expects home-cooked dinners, our social life planned, innovative sex, me to join him jogging, and God knows what else.

I feel totally frustrated.

STEVE: Laura keeps telling me that her work is important to her. She also has a lot of friends she's close to. I think it's great she's so involved. But where am I on her priority list? I'd like to be back toward the top like I was before. As things stand now, I feel closer to the bottom.

She keeps talking about balancing her life and organizing her time better. But if you look at what actually happens, there doesn't ever seem to be any time for *us*. Whenever I ask her to do anything — spend time by ourselves, make love, talk about what's going on in our respective lives, or, God forbid, cook dinner once in a while — she seems to resent it. And when she does agree, she's not really there. It's like she's doing me a favor.

6

Everything has become such a big deal. So more and more I'm just not asking. And that seems to suit her just fine. Frankly, I'm getting worn out by our hassles and by her constant anger. She's a wonderful woman. But I'm beginning to wonder if she's the wonderful woman for me.

Sound familiar?

Millions of men and women are wrestling at this very moment with just these kinds of issues, and these are men and women across the board — professional or working class, in two-career or traditional arrangements. Laura is typical of women who are out forging new paths for themselves. Steve is typical of the men who are of two minds about this.

Slow Changes in the Backwaters

To put it plainly, the New Male is a myth. (If you're a woman who has been looking for him, you may want to reconsider that particular search.) Pieces of the New Male exist, sure. (You're more likely to spot him in the early stages of courtship.) But the idea that there are lots of "whole" New Men out there, consistently, is wishful fiction. It's also way off the mark to think that there are lots of men out there today wishing and wanting to *become* New Men.

All of this is not to say that men aren't changing at all, or that there's a major backlash going on. There are some men who wonder if "things have gone too far." But, in my view, there is no going back. The revolution has happened, so to speak, and it's moving forward. It's just not finished yet. And it's just that men reside more in the backwaters of this massive revolutionary wave.

Men are moving far more slowly, quietly, and reluctantly than women. They're lagging behind. They're being pushed, pulled, and pressured every which way into a new future.

Remember, women are the active agents of change in all this. Men find themselves, perhaps for the first time in history, in the position of having to adapt. That responding position is a less than comfortable one for most men, accustomed as they are to initiating and being in charge. It's the rare individual who relinquishes privilege without resistance, however attractive the reasons for doing so might be.

The implications of men's having to divest themselves of power, or to redistribute it, to be exact, are enormous. Mostly, this rearrangement opens up far deeper issues for men today, issues seldom discussed, emotional issues that have to do with men's deep, long-standing, and largely *hidden* dependence upon the opposite sex. The American male's reluctance in the face of all the changes unfolding is intimately related to his ancient, largely unspoken need for the presence of women.

Alone in the Garden

Imagine our Adam, the first man, alone in the Garden of Eden, and you have a glimpse of how men are really feeling these days. If the major issue for women today is *overload* (balancing relationships, career, and if she's married, household, children, and all the rest), the crisis for men today is *loss* — the loss of women. At least, to men it feels like loss.

Women aren't available in the same ways as before, so men, in their hearts of hearts, are feeling let down, deserted, and keenly vulnerable to women's absence, whatever form that may take. Women remain mostly in the dark on this, because men aren't talking.

8

The other sex has pretty much always been duped into thinking that men need them *less* than they need men. That the reverse is more true is one of men's best-kept secrets. Men are much more dependent on women than women have even begun to realize. This is probably the most important thing for women to get through their heads about men, all seeming evidence to the contrary.

The next most important thing for women to understand and to accept is the many ways in which men are deeply different from them, for both biological and cultural reasons. Time and again, in trying to penetrate beneath that male inscrutability, women will mistakenly assume that men respond and feel as *they* do about many things. There is even more of a tendency now, in this "age of equality," to do this. Sameness between the sexes is emphasized as though differences have to mean problems. Well, differences *can* mean problems, but only when they are not properly understood. In fact, it's pretty much guaranteed they will be when that's the case. Assuming sameness when it doesn't exist, failing to recognize differences, is sure to lead to what I have come to call Perfect Misunderstandings between the sexes.

Our present-day Adams come to the sex-role revolution with an emotional landscape similar to women's, of course, but far from identical. Most men have few close bonds with anyone other than their lovers or partners (and perhaps their children). They value nurturing tremendously but usually have less skill than women in giving it. They are also less masterful than women at expressing their feelings and even at knowing them.

Most men *feel, fantasize, think,* and *act* very differently from women in regard to sex, intimacy, commitment, and all the rest that will be explored in the pages to come.

9

And men generally keep quiet about all of this.

It is from the quiet side of the sex-role revolution that I write this book. I break no sacred silences because, although most men go in disguise today, although most men run silent and deep when it comes to their feelings for women, at the same time they want very much to be understood. It is my intention to represent these feelings as best I can, at this particular moment in time, right in the thick of everything.

This book can be thought of as a communiqué from the male hideout, an interim report from the backwaters, from men in transition, in the process of changing. It is written, first, to women — to help you better understand the men you're loving or looking to love. It is written to men — to help you better understand yourselves and your part in the contemporary dance between the sexes.

Virtually all the men I see and talk with are either *in* a relationship or *looking* to be in one. So while this is a book about changes and differences, the need for intimate relationships with women has remained inviolate. We just somehow, together, have to weather the storm of shifting rules and expectations.

There has probably never been a harder time for relations between the sexes, and I expect that things won't settle down for some time to come. But if there's one thing I've learned from my many years as a psychologist, understanding is the first step to working things out.

II

In the Beginning

Twenty-five years ago, most women made hot breakfasts and packed lunches. They also laundered clothes and shopped for groceries and cleaned their houses. They took their children to school in the morning, then drove them to Boy Scout or Camp Fire Girl meetings or music lessons in the afternoon, and by five o'clock started to prepare dinner for a husband who came home from work.

Afternoons were spent tending preschoolers, shopping, ironing, scrubbing bathrooms, waxing floors, and, for women at the higher end of the economic spectrum, doing volunteer work or playing tennis with friends. Child-care centers served only the children of the poor. Women read Heloise, Doctor Spock, and magazines devoted to tips on sewing, cleaning, decorating, cooking, and "pleasing their husbands."

Twenty-five years ago, most men came home from a hard day at the office, factory, or department store, kissed their wives, had a drink, read the paper, ate

11

dinner, watched television, and maybe spent a little time with the children before bedtime. They washed cars, took out the garbage, and mowed the lawn on Saturday mornings. The family went for drives or had barbeques with friends and family on weekends.

Weekday nights, families watched television shows like *Father Knows Best, The Adventures of Ozzie and Harriet, Leave It to Beaver, The Donna Reed Show, The Lucy Show.* These gave us images of family life perfected (with a few breakfast-cereal commercials thrown in). They reinforced what boys and girls were already learning from parents about how men and women behave and how they relate to one another.

Women served, supported, sustained, and kept things together in the home. Men reigned, regulated, and seemed to be in charge inside *and* outside the home.

Women were demure. Men were heroic.

Men made money. Women spent it.

In all matters of major expenditures, however, men made the decisions. Men filed the tax returns and gave their wives an allowance to run the household and pay the bills. When the banker or life insurance agent called, women were sure to refer him to their husbands.

Women who worked outside the home did so as schoolteachers, nurses, saleswomen, secretaries, and librarians — only, or almost only. They took orders from men who were principals, doctors, managers.

Married women who had children and weren't poor rarely worked outside the home for pay. If they did, it was usually in part-time jobs for minimum wage, at hours compatible with their primary roles of wife, mother, and housekeeper. Most women's work provided no medical benefits or retirement plans. These needs, it was assumed, were "taken care of" by the male head of household. Employed or not, women were focused first on their families — their husband, their children, and all the intricate inner workings of the home. Only single women seemed to have careers, careers in a limited number of women's fields.

Twenty-five years ago, most people got married and expected to stay married — to the same person. They married young and had children immediately. Men came home to warm meals, clean houses, starched shirts, matched socks in the drawers, and scrubbed children (who were tired of dealing with Mom and eager to play with Dad). Men also came home — and this is key — to the devotion of an attentive wife, attentive in the domestic, emotional, and sexual spheres. Husbands were discreet if they had affairs, expected their spouses to be faithful, and felt somewhat reassured by their wives' apparent sexual naïveté.

All in all, you could say that men had it pretty good in those days.

That was life in the United States not so very long ago. Okay, maybe it wasn't *exactly* that way — but that's certainly the way the world was portrayed back then. That's the way we remember it.

Today, these descriptions sound absurdly out of date to most of us (nostalgically out of date to some). Nearly every detail of that earlier domestic picture has become obsolete. Less than 7 percent of today's American households include the lone breadwinning father, the full-time homemaking mother, and two children. The shift has been so fast that it seems more like a century's than just a quarter-century's worth of changes.

We're all, men and women alike, still reeling — albeit for radically different reasons and with little synchrony. The sexes aren't exactly waltzing smoothly together through the whole sex-role revolution. It's more of an un-dance, with women and men in different step.

This is because, contrary to popular mythology, things haven't changed equally on both sides. It's *women* who have changed. Everything else, everything men are having to deal with, originates in that palpable fact.

Here's what things look like for women now, as we approach the 1990s.

Women are spending their time differently.

Today, the vast majority of women — married or single, young or old, with or without children — works outside the home. The home front will never be the same as a result. Women's priorities have been rearranged. That's not to deny that many women are now caught doing double duty, as both workers *and* homemakers. But housekeeping and parenting are permanently out of the female closet and on the negotiating table of shared responsibilities between men and women. (Much more on these newly bewildering subjects later.)

More women than ever before are working, and more women than ever before are working in professions and positions that were previously all male. More are entrepreneurs. Of course, there's still a long way to go. Women earn only sixty-four cents for every dollar that a man earns today. And women are underrepresented in corporate boardrooms and in Washington. But the trend toward equity in the workplace is unlikely to stop. The California Commission on the Status of Women predicts that only 10 percent of the women living today will *never* have to work outside the home for pay. Women make up more than half the work force already.

The personal rewards for women working are many: independence, self-esteem, challenge, fun, social and intellectual stimulation, a sense of participation, an added identity anchor. But most women work for the same basic reason men do: economic necessity and security.

Given that it takes two incomes these days to support a middle-class life-style that only one male wage earner supported before, marriage is no longer the economic salvation it once was for women. Marrying is unlikely to keep a woman out of the labor force. What's more, with one in two marriages ending in divorce and with no-fault divorce the norm, women have to be prepared to support themselves, and maybe children too. Lifetime spousal support is a dim memory.

But if marriage no longer holds the promise of economic security, neither is marriage any longer the absolute necessity it was, now that women have their own income resources. Because of this, more women are choosing to remain single, to remain single longer, and to return to singlehood if they've been married. This isn't to say that, given tight economic times, there's no financial incentive to team up. There is, on both sides. Women just have more room to maneuver now.

Bottom line, married or not, women are expected to be financially self-sufficient today. They are less dependent materially on men. They are home less. And when they are home, they may have brought work from the office back with them. (One man even told me that his wife brought a copying machine into the bedroom!) This represents an enormous change from the past.

Women are thinking and feeling about themselves differently.

Today, women's idea of themselves is tied far less tightly, less exclusively, to the identities of wife and mother, or *prospective* wife and mother. While these roles may still be important to a woman, they no longer define her entirely, as they did previously. She's unbound from the old restrictions of who she was supposed to be and what she was supposed to do.

This unbinding is dramatically evident in women of all ages, but especially in the younger women coming up. I see it firsthand in my own twenty-three-year-old daughter. In a period of three years, Erica left a safe university environment and went first to France and then, a year later, to Japan. In both countries, she learned the language, found work, made friends, and supported herself financially and emotionally. After France and Japan, she returned to college and decided to become a filmmaker. In the most straightforward way, she assembled an academic committee and successfully obtained funding on her own from two national agencies. As I work on this manuscript, she completes her first thirty-minute documentary film. Somewhere down the career line, I think she expects to be married and have children, too.

This young woman does these things with a kind of self-assurance and confidence that are startling for me to behold. Surely, these strengths would be no less impressive in a son, or in anyone for that matter. My daughter may not be typical, but there are many others like her, women in their twenties and on up. They are feeling *good* about themselves. They have a sense of their own future. They support the ERA, they rally behind Gloria Steinem and Betty Friedan, they vote for candidates who represent their concerns best, and their copies of *Ms.* arrive alongside *Fortune, Vogue,* and *American Health.*

Women are changing what they want and expect from their intimate relationships with men.
Women still want intimate relationships with men.

16

They want them as much as ever. That hasn't changed, in spite of the emphasis in the early women's movement on total self-sufficiency. Most women today want to marry. Most want to have children. They are simply more likely to do both later in life than they did in the sixties.

What has changed are women's expectations of men!

Today, most women want a relationship that's a partnership. They expect to share equally with their partners: power, financial resources and responsibility, housekeeping, parenting, and the care and tending of the relationship itself. They also expect men to want exactly the same thing. In fact, they think we do! They believe we will feel and act differently from the way their fathers did, for instance. "After all," women conclude, "we've changed, the world's changed, men have changed too, right?"

Wrong. Men have changed some, but not that much.

This Perfect Misunderstanding is precisely where the sea of contemporary relationships parts, leaving both sexes stranded and confused, on opposite and sometimes opposing shores.

When it comes to relationships today, the vast majority of men feel themselves stuck between a rock and a "soft" place. Women have pretty much refashioned themselves. Men, on the other hand, stand betwixt and between old and new definitions of who they are supposed to be and what they are supposed to be doing. And it's not clear that men have decided they want to go where today's world is pushing them.

To get a true picture of how things look for men today, we have to step back twenty-five years again.

In those days, a man's raison d'être was *to make it as a man*, and men knew what was required to do that.

Men were expected to

- go to school
- go on to work (there was nothing as masculine as working and making money)
- advance in a career (this meant making *more* money)
- work without interruption until age sixty or seventy and retire
- be strong and resolute (invulnerability was a potent measure of maleness).

Somewhere along this work continuum, men were also expected to

- marry and have children (the home was man's sanctuary, the wife the sustainer).

Men were not *expected to*

- clean houses
- wash clothes
- diaper babies
- cook meals
- be mutually nurturing yet individually self-sufficient
- be vulnerable, sensitive, and openly affectionate
- relocate because the woman in one's life got a promotion (she wasn't even working!).

Not only were men *not* expected to do these things, we wouldn't be making it as men if we did.

Okay, now back to the present.

Today, the entire bottom half of the male prescription above has been turned upside down. Not by men. By women. Our wives, girlfriends, and even mothers are putting it to us to respond. Sooner, not later!

Men are supposed to

18

- share power (share power?)
- share feelings (share feelings?)
- share the special woman in their life with her workplace, her friends, and her "time for herself"
- support enthusiastically her career aspirations, talent, success, assertiveness, and independence (no patronizing, competitiveness, or terror, please)
- parent actively
- participate equally and happily in housework.

Meanwhile, men still feel the urgency to work, to be successful, to marry, to be the bottom-line provider "should something happen," and to be strong, machismo strong. Our culture still makes little room for men's emotional expressiveness, in spite of all the talk to the contrary. And there are mixed signals coming from women. As journalist Gloria Emerson eloquently puts it in *Some American Men,* "At a time when women, with good reason, are asking men to make known their most guarded feelings, when we want them to love and raise babies and remember our birthdays, it is also required that they be the ones to rescue people in a burning building. And startle the dragons when they are heard in the dark."

Men are feeling nothing less than overwhelmed by all this. They're caught between worlds. They're being asked to adapt to one quite different from the world they grew up in, while many of the old rules still apply. Men are uncertain that they can change and be "successful" at the same time. Neither are they certain that women won't walk out, not needing men exactly as they once did.

Three things are clear:

- Men's notion of what it means to be a man is in transition.

19

- Men fear that they are losing women, or have already lost them.
- The average guy is keeping both of the above under wraps. He's hiding his feelings from women and, in many cases, they're even hidden from himself.

Many men today have come to recognize there are some payoffs for them in all this. The money worries and responsibilities are no longer theirs to carry alone. (That's a big one!) With children, most men don't want to make the mistakes their own fathers made. They want to be the strong *positive* parts of their fathers, but they don't want to be the distant dad, the worn-out dad, the unavailable dad. Neither do men want to have to be "tough" all the time, or have their jobs consume their life. Most men want more than conventional job success today.

If all this is part of having equal relationships with women, well, okay. Besides, men think to themselves, how could I possibly stand against the principle of equality?

So, intellectually, a large number of men are there. Emotionally, it's another story.

Men *say* they support the changes going on in women's lives. Men *believe* they do in many cases. But men *feel* for the most part otherwise. In that discrepancy originate all the muddles and miscommunications.

HE SAYS: Of course, I don't expect her to do everything. That was okay for my mother because she never worked. It's not okay for the woman I'm living with.

BUT HE'S FEELING: *I'm tired at night. I want somebody to come home to, some undivided attention, some love and support on the other end.*

HE SAYS: Equal relationship! Yes! Of course!
BUT HE'S FEELING: *As long as I am first among equals!*

HE SAYS: I'm really glad she got that promotion. We can use the money.
BUT HE'S FEELING: *Damn. In another year, she's going to be making more than I am. I wonder if she will stick around.*

HE SAYS: I know it's important that I be there for her. She has just as much stress and responsibility as I do. Maybe more.
BUT HE'S FEELING: *Is this what I want? Two separate lives, eating out all the time, making appointments to see each other, rushing from one thing to another? We have no quiet, uninterrupted time together.*

HE SAYS: Sharing all the decisions is great.
BUT HE'S FEELING: *Why does everything have to be a meeting, a debate, and finally resolution?*

HE SAYS: Going to school is a terrific idea. She'll knock them on their ass!
BUT HE'S FEELING: *She's always been a sucker for really bright men. What chance am I going to have competing with her professors? It's going to be "tea and sympathy" all over again. Only this time, backward.*

However hidden and unspoken the feeling side of things, the inconsistencies come through loud and clear, one way or another, and these are driving women crazy! And, actually, the inconsistencies are driving men crazy too.

Men are frustrated, confounded, irritated, and also embarrassed by their contrary feelings. The more liberal the man in his thinking, the more shocked he is at the signs of his own traditional stripes. He watches himself encourage his lover to be assertive, to stand up for herself, with the boss, with her friends, with her family. Then he watches himself be put off when she does the same with him. Her firmness seems stubbornness; her persistence, intransigence; her challenges, arguments; her questions, demands; her forcefulness, stridency. He wants to hear what she has to say, but doesn't like it when she fights for her point of view with him — and wins!

The tangle gets even tighter.

Men in general seldom feel it's appropriate to express *any* feelings that smack of uncertainty, vulnerability, or hurt. (That's not part of the male code and, as said before, while loosened, that code still holds.) On top of that, liberal or otherwise, men are feeling it's equally inappropriate, in fact risky, to have any doubts about the women's movement. So you get layers of bound feelings. You get inconsistent behavior.

And you get *anger* — the explosive or the seething kind.

Take Dan, for instance, a forty-year-old dentist:

My wife decided to go to graduate school, full time. She didn't consult me. She just did it! I don't see her anymore. She's up at five forty-five getting ready to leave by six forty-five. Even worse, she loves it. The kids are on my side. My wife just thinks we're funny.

She goes to class, comes home late, and goes to sleep. Sex is nonexistent! In the past tense! Part of my former life! My world is upside down. Honestly, I may be a latent chauvinist, but I don't deserve this. Why do *I* have to do all the adjusting?

Anger like Dan's is a socially sanctioned emotion for men, one of the few. It consolidates the bottled-up feelings of abandonment, rejection, sadness, disagreement, and all the rest into one.

Women end up seeing only the anger and not what lies beneath. Sometimes, oftentimes, the men don't know what lies beneath their anger either.

Most men say they are attempting to share feelings, be more sensitive, and take greater responsibility for intimacy. Most men want to be active parents and advocate a balance of male and female influence on their children. Men talk proudly to their friends about their wives' accomplishments. Yet they see an ever-growing number of expectations, and say they're having a hard time keeping up. Most men want to be able to respond to this changing world appropriately, but question whether in the final analysis things will really be better for them.

So we are at a point in history where many men and women are blaming each other for the problems they're experiencing.

SHE THINKS: *If only* he *would understand how difficult it is and just pitch in without being asked.*

HE THINKS: *If only* she *didn't expect so much of me.*

SHE THINKS: *If only* he *would stop being so upset every time I'm not available at a moment's notice.*

HE THINKS: *If only* she *would spend more time worrying about me, rather than everyone else.*

SHE THINKS: *If only* he *were more sensitive to*

what's going on in my life and not choose times when I'm most exhausted.

HE THINKS: *If only she seemed more interested in making love rather than adding it to her list of obligations.*

Each sees the other as at fault. But neither is to blame. It's not his fault. It's not hers. The problems are theirs to solve, together, but they come from a phenomenon that's much larger than any single relationship.

For men, it would be helpful to realize that women assume that men have changed and don't really know men's real reactions. For women, it would be helpful to realize that men's anger may mark a myriad of feelings. Men aren't being intentionally deceptive. They simply don't themselves comprehend the depth of their own ambivalence. It is from this vantage point of confused and muddled feelings that we shall explore the nuances of male-female relations.

III

Modern Love: Sex and Other Splendors

All revolutions are not without their pleasure zones. It's not always all hardship and struggle. The *sex-role* revolution has come to us hand in glove with the *sexual* revolution. (No, they are not exactly the same thing, but they are intimately related.) Love relations between the sexes have somehow been changing as dramatically as our more broadly social ones. Both landscapes, it seems, have erupted simultaneously.

Of course, sex retains its deep mysteriousness for both men and women. That hasn't changed. It's still explosive. It's still an area of raw vulnerability. (Sometimes it seems an emotional minefield to be tread watchfully, especially for the unattached.) But at least, to the extent sex is knowable, we've come a long way toward opening up the subject and understanding it better. The brown paper wrapping has been removed for the most part.

Of all the changes women have wrought (yes, women

are in the lead here too), there is none that pleases
men more. On this topic, there is no discrepancy between men's thoughts and feelings. With the exception
of a few rigid traditionalists, they love what's happened. In this regard, they certainly don't want to go
back to the good old days.

The Other Revolution

Remember the "good girl"?

In case you don't recall or if you're too young to have
known how things were back in the fifties (and even
early sixties), sexually speaking, being the good girl
meant not having slept with a boy until you married
him or at least until you were engaged. Good girls did
not have sex with casual dates or, if they did, they
certainly would never let on.

Back in those days of not-so-long ago, the dating
mores for girls and women dictated that sexual intimacy progress along a prescribed behavioral timetable.
There were strict rules about kissing, touching, and
"going all the way." A number of women, my wife in-
cluded, have enlightened me on this subject.

On the first date, a good girl would let a boy hold
her hand and put his arm around her, if she liked him.
If she *really* liked him, she might even let him kiss
her, lightly. If she allowed this, however, there was
always the nagging worry that he might think she was
"easy." The question of whether or not you kissed a
boy on the first date was a favorite topic of school slum-
ber parties and college dorm-room talk.

There were usually an equal number of arguments
for and against "first date kissing," leaving the issue
continuously unresolved. Each girl had to decide for
herself on a date-by-date basis, and that was pretty
rough going. Most girls considered kissing appropriate

sometime between the second and fourth dates, so long as it was not "French kissing." (Once again, in case you don't know or can't remember, French kissing was open-mouthed, deep-tongue kissing.) That was reserved for much later in the dating sequence. If you were Catholic or strongly monastic, of course, it was never in the cards, at least not before marriage.

Another hot topic of debate was "*what* a boy touched and *when*." Getting back to our timetable, after holding hands and having an arm around her shoulder, a girl then had to decide how close to her breast she would allow a date's hand to get. Some hands never got too far. Others did, but that was seen as a kind of major gift you gave to a boy you liked a lot. For the fifties girl, there was also a related "layer" question. Did you allow your boyfriend to touch your breast (a) on top of your sweater, (b) under the sweater but on top of your bra, or — this was real serious stuff — (c) under the bra?

Most "good girls" moved into passionate fondling and French kissing (but did not go "all the way") as an intermediate step at the time they were asked to "go steady." In many ways a girl needed public proof, such as a high school ring, a boy's varsity sweater, or a college fraternity pin to justify heavy petting. After all, engaging in such passionate behavior without some kind of visible commitment from a guy might lead to his publicly talking about "how far he got." Your reputation would be ruined. That was something all girls feared back then. In their own minds, a girl who was "easy" was someone reviled. A *bad* girl. The worst of the worst. Much worse than a bad *boy!*

As to when girls did go "all the way," for some this was put off until the wedding night. For others, a commitment of marriage with an engagement ring was sufficient. For most, I'm told, an absolute requirement

27

for making love was being "totally and thoroughly *in love* with him" — whoever he was. Many young women felt that "having sex" with a man was the same as committing to marry him. One did not do one without expecting the other.

Being a virgin, or having other people *think* you were a virgin, was a big deal in those days.

As to the dating ritual itself, whether you were a good girl or a bad girl (you could only be one or the other), the male did the asking. (He also did the paying.) A young woman would never dare to ask a young man out, except under *very* special circumstances. (And an older woman asking a young man out? Or going out with him on any basis? Unthinkable.)

Take high school twenty-five years ago. A girl asked a boy out *only* if the school she went to held a Sadie Hawkins Day (or a backward or turnabout) dance. This was a special, once-a-year event inspired by the comic-strip character Sadie Hawkins, who made an annual chase after Li'l Abner. In college, a girl could ask a boy out if her sorority or club or residence hall sponsored a dance. Asking was also okay for proms and special college weekends if the boy you wanted to go with wasn't enrolled in your school. If he was, you waited for him to ask you.

Other than in these situations, young school women never asked men out to do anything. And women once they were out of school rarely would ask a man out. A singles dance sponsored by a church, synagogue, or other such group might afford the occasional opportunity. Otherwise women sat and waited to be asked. For some girls, it wasn't even a matter of waiting to be asked. They waited to be noticed. That was their role. They waited at home. They waited at parties. Sometimes, they waited in bars.

For women in the unmarried state, and for the unmarried men who went out with them, that's pretty much how things were. Women didn't (or mostly didn't) have sex before marriage. They didn't initiate dates. And they didn't expect to pay for anything. They certainly didn't

- ask men out to dinner
- send men flowers
- go alone to restaurants, bars, or singles clubs to meet men
- invite men to spend the night with them
- expect to live with a man before marriage
- expect to make decisions about pregnancy
- expect to take responsibility for contraception
- expect to have multiple sexual partners
- expect to remain single after a certain age. (An unmarried twenty-five-year-old woman was feeling pretty panicked and on the verge of being "an old maid." Women didn't expect to live alone, unmarried, for any length of time. Or at least not happily so.)

Twenty-five years ago, unmarried *or* married, women didn't

- initiate sex
- expect to know very much about sex
- expect to have orgasms
- expect ever to be divorced.

Back into the Eighties

Now, twenty-five years later, women are doing all of those things — before, during, and *after* marriage — and they are doing them without fear of public censure. Women are much more open about their sexuality.

Only the rare woman today is a virgin before mar-

29

riage or outside of marriage. Being a good girl or a bad girl is not an issue (except for those with strong religious values).

Women are seeking pleasure in *their own right* from sex. For women, sex is no longer tied to duty, on the one hand, or pretensions of not enjoying it, on the other. Nor does sex have to mean pregnancy if you don't want it to.

The male orgasm is no longer the main event. Now there are two.

Women are initiating sex.

Women are suggesting sexual experimentation.

These are the primary pieces of the modern sexual ground on which we find ourselves standing today. No longer are sexual relationships defined by what a man wants, needs, and expects from a woman. She brings her own set of wants, needs, and expectations to things now. As a result of all this, we're seeing our newfangled notion of shared responsibilities extending itself into yet another dimension of relations between the sexes, the dimension of lovemaking and the dating dance. Things are no longer all *for* the man. But neither are they all *up to* him now.

Today's Woman

Let's take a closer look at these changes, beginning with *premarital sex.*

When you think about it, just the term "premarital sex" sounds old-fashioned, even archaic. It conveys the disapproval of a bygone era. As a phrase, it's gone the way of the black-and-white TV, still around but seldom put to use. It can't compete with the reality that we are now in.

For a single woman today, whether she has been married or not, sexual activity is more or less an ac-

cepted and healthy part of dating or seeing a man.
Family upbringing, religious beliefs, and just life experience will influence an individual woman's attitude
toward this. A handful of women may still be "saving
themselves for marriage," for instance. (I venture to
say that most young women would find that idea amus-
ing.) But for the vast majority of women, sex before
marriage is exceedingly normal behavior. In fact, many
women say they feel it's *expected.*

Young women tell me that not having sexual experience is seen by the men they date as a real negative. In fact, one high-schooler said that she had been
one of three virgins in her graduating class and "that
was really embarrassing." Young women also tell me,
particularly those in high school and college, "The minute you say you'll go out with a guy, you are automatically expected to sleep with him." So some choose
not to date. More and more women, however, at younger
and younger ages, are choosing to have sex with their
dates or boyfriends, in spite of the new complicating
pressures. Unattached women in their twenties and
thirties may have two or three ongoing sexual relationships at once, as men have always done. It may not
be the rule, but neither is it the exception.

With contraception no longer a taboo subject and
contraceptive measures readily available today, most
women can separate the issues of sexuality and pregnancy. The possibility of getting pregnant can recede
into the distant background of lovemaking if a woman
so chooses. The eighties woman takes active responsibility for this and for not getting pregnant, unlike
women in the fifties who left contraception up to the
man (who carried an ever-ready condom in his wallet
until it disintegrated and was replaced by another).
Now a man has a test to pass. If he doesn't ask a woman
if she's protected, *and* what birth control she's using,

he's uncaring. If he does ask, he cares, about me and about "us," a woman thinks. Most men don't know about this test, and they fail it.

Unlike their mothers, many women today aren't waiting, or at least not all the time, for their men or their dates to ask for sex. They are quite willing to ask for it themselves, feeling good about doing that. Increasing numbers of American women are viewing sex as an integral and natural part of expressing affection in a relationship, early on. Increasing numbers of *married* women are taking sexual partners outside of marriage. The "open marriage" phase of the sixties is behind us, but infidelity is still an issue, only now for women as well as for men.

Single or married, most women today are more knowledgeable about sex, and sex has become more of a personal priority than it once was, or once was allowed to be. Variety, playfulness, and experimentation are all important to women, who may just be the one to bring home the X-rated video for a special evening. They do not view sex as an obligation (or mostly don't), but rather as an opportunity for pleasure and gratification — theirs and their partners'. Lovemaking has been profoundly affected by all this.

And what about changes in *dating*? Aside from the inclusion of sex that I've just sketched?

Well, first of all, unlike "premarital sex," the term "dating" seems to have somehow survived into the last half of the eighties. (I guess we couldn't come up with a better one.) Dating continues to describe all the activities involved in "going out" with a member of the opposite sex. The word is the same, but the rules of the game have changed. And they are still changing. The contemporary date bears little resemblance to its predecessor.

It is not unusual for a woman to ask a man to go out

with her now. How comfortable she is doing that will be pretty much related to her level of self-esteem, and her age. (The higher her self-esteem, the lower her age, the more likely she is to ask.) Nor is it unusual for a woman to pay. Twenty-five years ago women never paid for anything except in those special circumstances described earlier. Today, one of the unwritten rules of dating, particularly among employed women (less so of high school and college girls) is "you ask, you pay," or at minimum you go "Dutch," each paying for himself and herself.

Today's woman usually carries a series of her own charge cards and doesn't feel at all hesitant about using them. She usually tries to anticipate how a man will feel about the paying issue and then acts appropriately, trying neither to overwhelm him nor to insult him. First and second dates tend to be the stickiest. Then as the couple gets to know each other, if things proceed, it gets easier to figure out who pays what, based on the financial resources each brings to the dating situation.

Some women actually prefer doing the asking and the paying, regardless of their financial status, because they feel this gives them more control over the dating situation, particularly the sexual dimension. Kate, a twenty-seven-year-old graduate student, expressed this to me:

> When I ask a man to do something, let's say to go to a play, and I pay for it or we go "Dutch," I don't feel nearly as obligated to sleep with him at the end of the evening as when he asks me out and drops $100 on dinner and the theater. I feel like I can say yes or no without guilt.

As I watch this young woman making her way skillfully through all the unknowns of this relatively new sexual territory, I know there are many others just like her today, women of all ages, drafting the roadmaps as they go. Men are exploring also, and sometimes their paths are not exactly the same.

The Male Side

When it comes to dating, most men say they are happy with the new balance. They seem to mean it. They like the reciprocity, and they enjoy being asked and even pursued at times. They talk about how much less game playing there is today and how reasonable it is that *she* call him, rather than its always being the other way around. Men also say it's useful for *her* to understand the anxiety about rejection that men have been experiencing for years as they picked up the phone to call *her* for the first date.

For younger men still in school, the alternating of asking seems natural since they've known no other way. For men in their thirties and forties, it's still somewhat surprising to be approached at a party, called on the phone, and have *her* invite *him* out for a non-business lunch. Many men still stammer when asked for their number by an attractive woman and frequently will respond with a business card rather than a home phone number. They are more used to that.

Other men, particularly those in their forties and beyond, *say* they like the change too, but they *feel* different. They still like being the one in charge, enjoy being the pursuer, and feel put off if a woman calls, or calls very often. They use words like "pushy," "aggressive," and even "unfeminine" to describe women who seem to come on too strong. They still have needs for the old kind of power and may even lose interest if a woman is too persistent.

With regard to finances, there is less ambivalence. Single men acknowledge the fairness of her sharing expenses, particularly since she's likely to be self-supporting and may have a disposable income that is even greater than his. Very often trips or vacations are planned with frank discussions about who will be paying for what. Many couples — dating, married, living together, or whatever — actively engage in ongoing financial negotiations that are much more open than their own parents ever dreamed of.

There are still some men, particularly those in their forties and fifties, who feel that it is their place to pick up the check. Others say they expect a woman to be willing to pay her fair share, even though they won't ultimately accept her offer to do so. It's the principle with them, not the money.

Women have to be pretty agile to deal with this panoply of responses. Some men like to be called, others don't. Some men expect to share expenses, others seem insulted by this. It's not that men are trying to be difficult. Most, as I said, like where things are going. It's just the usual confused fallout of familiar patterns in flux.

There is some of the same when it comes to the changes in everything having to do with lovemaking. Confusion comes part and parcel with the times. But, all in all, there are very few men who aren't pleased that the old torturous sexual timetable has been abandoned.

Men today, and that includes younger men (dating girls still in high school), simply assume that the women or girls they date are not virgins (incidentally, that doesn't translate as "bad girls" now). Almost without thinking, it's taken for granted that sex is likely to be a part of going out together, sooner rather than later. In this day and age, it would be highly out of the ordinary for a man to marry in order to gain a steady sexual partner. (That's what men used to do, believe it or not.)

Of course, there are some out there, not necessarily white-haired but with a little bit of gray, who managed to miss the sexual revolution because they have remained faithful in their traditional marriages for the last twenty years or so. Men like this who reenter singlehood now, for one reason or another, feel initially overwhelmed. The sexual opportunities seem staggering to them. But usually after some early apprehension about their own performance, and maybe some frenzied sexual activity too, most come happily and moderately to terms with the new state of affairs.

Men of all ages have a need to "score." (More will be said on this later.) And there are still some men who tell locker-room stories about their sexual exploits. However, since most men and women are sexually active today, conversations about who's doing what with whom have lost their sizzle. Once the turbulence of adolescence is left behind, it is rare to hear adjectives like "fast" or "easy" ascribed to a sexually active woman.

Both outside and inside marriage, men are liking the fact that they are no longer solely responsible for initiating lovemaking and for varying the lovemaking repertoire. This is especially true of long-standing relationships, but it's also true for those first encounters. If there's a basic attraction, by and large, men respond readily to women's advances and sexual expressiveness. Her suggesting "let's try something different tonight" brings a smile of anticipation rather than a disapproving look. Her invitation for a weekend away for just the two of them is warmly received. That's how most men feel.

There is a smaller group having some problems with

36

this, particularly within marriage. Men who are themselves sexually inhibited or who have high needs for
control may still see the domain of sexual initiation as
theirs. They may still want to control both the frequency and the pace of lovemaking with their partner.
This is the minority position, however. Men and women
in their second marriages are saying how much more
sexually gratifying their new relationships are, not being
burdened as their first marriages were with the old
expectations of sexual passivity in women.

Lest this all sound too good to be true, there is some
trouble in the married sector over the issue of extramarital sex — extramarital sex on the woman's part.
Married women's increasing sexual activity outside of
the conjugal bedroom elicits a strong, negative response from most married men. Men still have a double
standard when it comes to infidelity. And even other
women are likely to judge a woman's infidelity more
harshly than a man's.

When it comes to their own behavior, men are much
more sexually liberated, and have been for some time.
When it comes to their partners, husbands are more
likely to leave if "she's fooling around." It likely has
to do with women's greater linking of sexuality with
intimacy and the long-standing image of the wimpy
male cuckold.

Finally, on the subject of men's responses, I'd like to
put to rest the rumor that an epidemic of impotence
has risen up in the face of women's growing sexual
assertiveness. Surely, issues of power and control influence men's relations with women (as they do their
relations with other men). To be in a relationship with
a woman who is sexually experienced, or *more* sexually
experienced, initially can be distressing. ("She's been
with other men. I may not be powerful enough for her.")
But there's no evidence that men generally are having

more problems with sexual potency with respect to any of this. (That goes for older men too.) What's occurred is that impotence, like other sexual problems, is now talked about openly, or more openly than before.

Exclusive Arrangements

Let's double back to the modern dating scene and see what happens from there these days.

In the past, dating was more or less the first act in a three-act drama that lowered the curtain with marriage. Courtship was Act Two. Unless one was a "spinster" or "confirmed bachelor," everybody more or less followed that sequence of settling down with the opposite sex. Women might be eighteen or nineteen (twenty-one or twenty-two if they went to college) and men not a lot older at the time they "tied the knot."

Today, dating is still Act One, but everything after that is improvisation, as they say in the theater. There's also the possibility of a whole new act, Living Together, that may be the final act for a couple. They may or may not go on to marriage.

It goes something like this now.

You start going out regularly but not exclusively. (That's the search.)

You start going out exclusively. (This is testing.)

You decide to live together. Now things get complicated. This can mean one, or both, of two things: a commitment to stay together for a time that isn't seen as forever, or a commitment to stay together for a time that *is* seen as forever, however "forever" shakes down. (More testing.)

You decide to marry. This is definitely a forever step, divorce statistics notwithstanding, and it's *still* the most common one. Courting can occur before living together as well as before marrying. And you can check out at any point along the way and start all over with someone else.

What's happened, in essence, is that a larger space has been carved out for nonmarried life. Marriage is a long ways from being an anachronistic institution. But the premarital turf has expanded enormously, as has the postmarital and never-marital ground, for both sexes.

Women and Marriage

On the female side of things, heretofore only the most unusual woman approached marriage as an option. Only the most bohemian would have dared to live openly with a lover. Certainly no woman in her right mind delayed getting married to launch a career, except perhaps if she were a movie star. And not even movie stars forwent marriage altogether.

Now, in most circles, there is little or no stigma attached to a woman's remaining single, for however long, even lifelong, although most women still marry eventually. Some of our most famous American women are notably single by choice. Gloria Steinem, Jacqueline Onassis, and Katharine Hepburn come readily to mind. These are role models for a whole new pattern of singlehood for women. Many women are waiting until their late twenties to begin thinking about marriage. Most of the time, these delays are made in the name of getting a career firmly off the ground.

A woman is likely to choose to live with a man during this time, however. In many ways, living together has become a substitute for an early first marriage. In fact, it's almost expected.

Bianca, a thirty-two-year-old executive secretary, told me, "I think guys expect you to have lived with some-

one *before* them. You know, they want to be with someone who knows their way around."

All of the above having been said, after a period of
singleness that is highly likely to have been longer
than their mothers', most women today want an ongoing, stable relationship with one man that they hope
will culminate in marriage. They may be living with
him, but they want ultimately to live with him married.

Age thirty, give or take some years on either side,
is about the time that women begin to feel the desire
to settle down and have a family. This is roughly the
time that men start wanting the same thing. Only they
often want it a little less urgently. Young men don't
have the two time barriers facing them that young
women do. The first is fixed and biological. That's having children. The second is less fixed and social. That's
the shrinking pool of available men as women grow
older in this society. Here are some recent figures:

- Chances that a white, college-educated twenty-five-
  year-old woman will marry: 1 in 2.
- Chances that a white, college-educated thirty-five-
  year-old woman will marry: 1 in 18. (Statistics are
  similar for women of color.)

These realities are producing heretofore unthinkable behaviors: women dating much younger men, women
increasingly dating married men, and women having
children on their own.

The numbers problem is not a given like the natural
limit on childbearing. The shortage of eligible men for
women in their thirties and on up is a shortage that's
been created by another double standard, the double
standard of aging. Those same attributes that *increase*
a man's marriageability as he ages *decrease* a woman's.

40

Men who are older, richer, brighter, more powerful, more successful, and more attractive have a *great* number of women to choose from. Women who become richer, smarter, more powerful, and more successful over time have a *meager* number of potential partners to choose from. Only a woman's attractiveness seems to link positively with desirability.

But even there, as we all know, her attractiveness is called into question as she ages. A man gets character lines. A woman gets wrinkles. Gray hair makes him look distinguished and her drab. Women continue to be prized in this society first for their attractiveness, an attractiveness based primarily on youth. This is an area that is changing for women, but at a relative snail's pace. In the meantime, older, accomplished, and powerful women still find themselves discarded or passed over for "younger models."

So, as single women move into their thirties, forties, and fifties, finding that stable ongoing relationship becomes more difficult. And as the pool of men becomes smaller, so do the chances of finding a man who shares expectations of an "egalitarian" relationship. On the one hand, women are fairly comfortable delaying marriage. On the other, because everything hasn't changed yet, they're discovering that this delay can be risky *if* what they want is to be *married.*

So women are having to steer a wise course between singlehood and marriage these days. They do this knowing that, given a fifty percent divorce rate, they can't expect marriage will necessarily meet their financial and emotional needs anyway, at least not forever. Single women today are deeply reluctant to emulate their mothers who devoted themselves fully to finding the right man, to the exclusion of all else.

Men and Marriage

On the male side of things, the vast majority of men want to marry, and they really do want the marriage to be forever. (This goes even for the previously married.)

At the same time, most men seem pleased by the seeming lack of pressure for early marriage. They say they like to be with women who are less focused on "where this relationship is going." Many men say they have no intention of marrying early. They like playing the field. They are much more casual about living with a woman and *don't* see this as a permanent commitment necessarily, and certainly not as a proposal. They would laugh at the suggestion that they had to get married in order to have sex.

Men are, however, somewhat suspicious about *her* liberalism when it comes to these arrangements. They question just how relaxed she is about things like commitment and whether her freedom and financial independence are real. Men talk with one another about the friend who married a woman with a $30,000-a-year job but who then told him that she really didn't expect to go on working "forever."

Men are very apprehensive about the financial consequences of marriage. Many men see a prenuptial agreement as mandatory, but also worry about whether (if push comes to shove) it will really protect them. Every man has a friend who talks about having been "taken to the cleaners," in spite of no-fault divorce, and divorced men in particular seem reluctant to risk their financial independence again. Few women, even those with assets, understand how widespread this financial anxiety is.

These fiscal cautions aside, paradoxically, most men feel uncomfortable with women who seem *too* self-sufficient. They look for women who seem to need as well as want them. Secretly, many men want a woman who leans toward the traditional in her attitudes about marriage and wants to create a home for him.

Some men express a concern about being seen by women as "breeders." They feel somewhat apprehensive of a woman with a loudly ticking biological clock. They don't want to marry only because she wants to have children, particularly if she seems adamant about his taking on an equal-parenting role. Men still want to feel that they are the askers. They don't respond very well to proposals of marriage.

Perhaps in this area not so much has changed. Men still want to marry a woman they are "in love with," and who they feel loves them. However, their expectations of what a marital relationship should be is perhaps not quite what *she* has in mind. While the new woman may be looking for the new man, often the issue of men's willingness to commit is a question of committing to what — what she expects, or what he truly wants? These, of course, may not always be the same thing.

Commitment

Commitment is one of those loaded words between the sexes that many a relationship, or budding relationship, has run aground on. In the old days, it wasn't such an issue because you either got married or you didn't, and marriage was synonymous with commitment. You somehow always knew where you stood. He either called back or he didn't, he proposed or he didn't. She either said "yes" or said "no" ("maybe" was okay for a few days). Today, with a wider field of commitment possibilities, and not all of them of the forever kind, there's a sea of uneasiness between the sexes, and the uneasiness is mostly on women's part. Commitment is deeply important to both sexes, but men and women come to it just differently enough that they sometimes miss each other. Sometimes a flood of mistrust and misunderstanding rushes into that crack of difference. And the waters can begin to rise as early as the close of the first date.

Disparate Fantasies

Jane is a twenty-nine-year-old single woman who had recently gotten her MBA and was in the midst of choosing among several impressive job offers. Along with finding the right job, she had decided that with school behind her, she wanted to find the right relationship too. It seemed like the time to do that. One of her close male friends, in whom she had confided about this, had someone he wanted her to meet, someone he thought she'd be crazy about — successful, good-looking, slightly buttoned-down, mid-thirties, and *available*. Her number was given to this guy, he called, and they arranged to meet for a late-afternoon drink a few weekdays later. He sounded appealing to Jane over the phone. She tried to keep her expectations at bay (but she had already begun a "what if" trip).

Well, he *was* everything her friend had said and she *did* find him attractive. (Blind meetings aren't always this auspicious.) But there was a problem. After forty minutes of the kind of conversation you have when first getting to know someone, someone of the other gender, he put his napkin down on the table and said he'd have to be going. Too shocked to protest, Jane stood up as he did, they walked to the entrance together, exchanged a superficially pleasant good-bye, with no words about getting together again, and walked to their separate cars.

44

Jane was incensed at his rudeness. (She hadn't even finished her drink.) But what she really felt was, "What happened? Wasn't I his type? What was that all about, just a quick once-over?"

Alexandra, Alex for short, is another single woman, age thirty-four, an accomplished writer. She had lived with two different men in the past, and had never been married. She was between relationships now and was beginning to long for the next one to be the real, lasting thing. She had been seeing a number of men, but not sleeping with any of them, not really wanting to. Then she met Geoff, a professor of music, a virtuoso pianist, forty-one, and previously married. This was no ordinary classical musician. This man was electric, or so thought Alex. ("Now, here's a possibility. We'll make love to Mozart, many times, passionately.")

They started to see a fair amount of one another over the next few weeks. There was lots of "chemistry" and mutual excitement. He was talking about trips they might take together that summer. ("So he's thinking about the future too!") Toward the end of the month, they made love for the first time, one night at Alex's place. (The waiting had made it all the more special, Alex thought, and it was pretty nice for the first time.) They had fallen asleep when, sometime past midnight, Alex awoke to find Geoff putting on his clothes.

"You're not leaving, are you?"

"Yes, I've got a lot to do tomorrow." (Tomorrow was Saturday.)

"But I thought we'd spend the night together. We just made love. How can you go so soon? I thought you'd want to stay."

Well, he stayed. But the next morning as he was leaving, Alex found herself feeling suddenly uneasy, wondering when she'd see him again, wondering why he hadn't said he wanted to see her again as soon as possible — that night, in fact. ("After all, it is Saturday night, and he can't be working then, can he?") He said, warmly, that he'd call. She felt abandoned. He did call — on Tuesday. They continued to see each other for a little while longer. They even slept together again. But it was never the same.

Elizabeth is a forty-three-year-old woman who is newly divorced, her choice. She owns her own business and thrives on hard work. She'd like to have an intimate partner, but that doesn't have to mean marriage, necessarily, this time.

Recently, at a party with friends, she met a man about her age, who told her early on in the evening that he found her very attractive and would love to make love to her. She felt taken aback by this, but thought to herself, "Well, at least there's no confusion. None of this spending hours drinking and so on as the customary prelude to his making a move at the end of the evening. This guy said what he wanted right up front. And he seems nice." Still, what he was suggesting wasn't exactly her style. So even though she found him attractive too, she gently declined. He graciously accepted, or seemed to.

Later, at home, as she was ruminating in bed over whether she'd been foolish to turn him down, the phone rang. It was him.

"Look, I've got some cognac and chocolate here. Why not come over? We can just talk. I'd like to get to know you better."

"But it's eleven thirty! I wouldn't be much company at this late hour."

"Come anyway. I'd really like to see you."

Well, she ended up telling him "no" for the second time that night and wondering again as she fell asleep

46

whether all that had been a line. "How do you know? What are men thinking? What's going on out here?"

The "out here" is singlehood.

None of the men that Jane, Alex, and Elizabeth encountered in these stories was trying to be Mr. Heartbreak (although, clearly, the first seemed not to have the vaguest acquaintance with the chivalric code). Yet each woman in this trio, and these are strong women, felt in her own way in some emotional jeopardy. The men were uneasy too, but for different reasons. Let's take our privileged observer's look at their side, beginning with Jane's blind date, David.

For David, it was simple. Jane just didn't come across to him as warm or responsive. When he moved his chair slightly closer to hers as they sat down, she stiffened. She smiled but then moved her hand away quickly when his accidentally brushed hers. All in all, in that first impression, she just didn't seem to be very interested. And he wasn't going to pursue it, even though he was attracted to her. Why spend a lot of time trying to begin something when it was clear to him she didn't want to get close? In this case, he had blown it. Indeed, Jane was both interested and interesting. But David could not tolerate the anxiety of waiting to find that out. He bolted before having invested anything.

Geoff's situation was more complicated. Alex thought his going to leave without staying the night was a rejection of her. It wasn't really. He truly did have something to do the next morning. He had enjoyed their lovemaking. He too felt it had been pretty good, for the first time. But Geoff, at this time in his life, was not interested in a committed relationship. His divorce wasn't a bad one. But he simply didn't want an exclusive arrangement that promised more down the road. By talking about the future, Geoff hadn't felt he was "making a commitment." He was simply thinking ahead to summer activities he and Alex might want to do together. As he sensed her uneasiness and anxiety that night, he began to pull back. He didn't tell her what was going on, of course. But, behaviorally, he just withdrew.

Elizabeth's man, Alan, charming and married twice before, was simply interested in a one-night stand. Since the direct approach hadn't worked, he called back and tried to pull off another, using the sensitive-man approach. Elizabeth was right in being concerned that it was simply a line. It was. But it was a pretty good one — and left her wondering.

More often than not, even at the beginning, the sexes can be at cross-purposes without their even realizing it. For that complex of cultural and biological reasons, each brings to the mating-dating dance related but disparate fantasies. Men and women approach these first encounters deeply differently as a result.

The *primal female fantasy* goes something like this. Prince Charming comes (an executive on Wall Street, an artist who's up and coming, the guy in the apartment next door). He's smitten by her, loves her, perhaps doesn't rescue her if her life isn't so bad but surely transports her to some transcendent region of feeling, and commits to her early on. (Of course, he's willing to do his share of sweeping out the castle.) Sometime after she feels emotionally bonded (an hour, a day, a week), or something akin to emotional bonding, they can make love.

The *primal male fantasy* is more like this. Dream Girl comes, or maybe he goes to her (an attractive, but not too beautiful, executive on Wall Street, artist who's up and coming, woman next door). She responds to him physically early on. She takes his hand, for instance, moves close when he puts his arm around her, and in all those little body-language ways lets him know that

48

soon (an hour, a day, a week), they will become lovers, or something akin to lovers. Then (and only then) can he begin to open up emotionally.

A man doesn't literally need to score straightaway, but he needs some degree of sexual acceptance before even thinking about relationship concerns. He can't begin connecting until this is taken care of. A woman doesn't literally need a commitment straightaway, but she needs some degree of closeness, even a fantasy of closeness, as a precursor to sex. This is not to say there aren't times when women want sex for sex's sake. But the one-night stand and the "zipless fuck" are not the preferred seductive fare these days, for women or for men.

In spite of all that's changed with respect to sexual behavior, especially for women, the female *commitment* imperative and the male *scoring* imperative, or at least remnants of these imperatives, still seem to be hanging around in our respective psyches. Once these are assuaged, early on, a man and a woman can get on with the business of seeing whether there's any basis for a real relationship.

A man and a woman who don't make it that far have usually crashed upon the barrier reef of those first primal differences. Those who pass through, however rocky the passage, usually do so by navigating instinctively, with a certain hardiness and, if they're lucky, with the benefit of prior experience, recognizing this temporary phase for what it is. Others who tend to bolt at the earliest sign of asymmetry need to steady themselves with as much information as they can get about those initial primal contraries. The basic ones have been described. Here are some elaborations.

- For men, by and large, sex = sex, like X = X. They can separate sex from feelings far more easily than women can, in the beginning. (A man may really want nothing more in a particular situation, like Alan above.)

- For women, by and large, sex = sex and. For them, it's more like X = X + Y; the Y stands for feelings. Sex and feelings are much more intricately linked, from the beginning (as they were for Elizabeth).
- Women feel more at risk with sex. Men feel more at risk with dependency.
- He's trying to score — or at least be assured she "wants" him. She's trying to keep from feeling used — or at least be assured he "cares" for her.
- Men don't talk about being used, or rarely do. (*If it feels this good getting used, then use me up.*) Men are flattered if a relative stranger propositions them at a party. (*She can put her shoes under my bed anytime.*)
- Women talk about being used all the time. (*Is he lying? Does he like me or does he just want to score?*) They may be somewhat flattered at a stranger's proposition, but it will also cross their minds to be insulted. (Refrain: *Does he like me or just want to score?*)

On both sides, there is no solution but to understand all this — to understand, first, yourself and, next, the other. The idea is to take the sexual tension and make it work for you, much the way actors develop personal methods for making the tension of performance work for them. If you think about it, if there weren't any tension, there wouldn't be much to respond to, in any way. Both sexes really want someone they have to deal with, positively.

At the early stages of getting to know a man, most women go wrong by tending to give too much importance to "the relationship" long before it's appropriate.

They begin to think something is there before it's really had a chance to develop.

Men go wrong by holding back too long. Often, by the time they become ready to be emotionally vulnerable, a woman is feeling frustrated and exhausted.

In recent years, in our modern sexual climate, I've observed many single women thinking that they are somehow wrong to place such high value on relationship. So they do all sorts of things, usually counterproductive things, to pull that value in and to pull themselves in. But it's the timing, not the value itself, that needs care. Valuing a relationship is wonderful. Besides, ultimately, it's what men want too. In the same way that women don't want to be used, men don't want to be number 17 on Wednesday night either. A man also likes to feel chosen for himself and would like to see a good thing last. Only a small subsegment either don't want or can't tolerate, for a multitude of reasons, intimate relationships with women.

Most men come to commitment a little more slowly than women because they feel more at risk. Men walk their own delicate line when it comes to relationships. "I want to be needed, but not pressured." So they give lots of confusing, cautionary messages of the "go away a little closer" kind.

For men, commitment is spelled *responsibility*. It's the old ball and chain, which gets hooked onto men, not women. It's not so much that men fear sexual chains, although a man might feel that way at first. Rather, it's that you're chained to a whole different world than the one you inhabited when you were single or not living with anyone. This is a world in which you will *always* feel responsible for your partner and for possible children, even if she's making lots of money. She could quit at any time. You'll get wiped out.

51

Men's thoughts follow this kind of progression when it comes to commitment. This is a logic that women don't relate to *at all*. This is an issue that men think about *all the time*. It's also an issue that men are actively grappling with today.

As a society, we have passed through the promiscuity, open marriage, and "who is this next to me" phases of the sixties and seventies. An epidemic of sexually transmitted diseases like herpes and AIDS has intervened. That partly explains the change, but only partly. Serial relationships have emotional as well as physical costs. Sex is much more likely today to happen between men and women who know one another, and know one another well. People are wanting now to settle down. Commitment is "in," or back in — in new ways. All of us are in the midst of redefining relationships. We have no one to point the way. So we're teaching ourselves and teaching each other as we go.

First dates and first infatuations are just the beginning. Navigating through modern courtship comes next.

IV

Modern Love: Beyond Infatuation

♦

Let's say you have made it through the straits of dating and you are now seeing someone regularly and exclusively. The search is over, forever or at least for a time. You have come to some accord on the relationship issue (you both need and want the other in your life), and you are now in a deeper phase of testing and, as you continue to get closer, courting — courting as a prelude to living together or to marrying.

Considering the times we live in, the phenomenon of courtship itself has remained remarkably intact. The dictionary defines it as "paying respectful and flattering attention to in order to get the love of." Well, that's still how it goes. It's also still the case, and by now this should come as no surprise, that men and women come to courting with that usual hair space of difference.

Women tell me that courtship is the time when men are the most verbal, open, caring, understanding, tender, and communicative. Unlike any other time in their lives, courting men take long romantic walks on beaches and city streets and spend long languorous hours in bed. They stay up until two in the morning sharing their hopes, fears, and dreams and listening to the same for their loved ones. Driven by strong emotions and powerful sexual feelings, men often become more of, well, everything during this time.

Men send love notes, give gifts (little and big), buy flowers, make thoughtful gestures, and even anticipate their lovers' every need. A courting man enthusiastically shares the cooking *and* the dishes afterward. He is interested in his lover's work and seems understanding when she is occasionally late from an office meeting that dragged on. He talks about women having the same right to succeed as men. He is solicitous when his lover is bushed.

Many a woman views such courtship behavior by her man as the major predictor of their future "happily ever after" life together. She thinks the way he is now will be the way he will be forever! What a guy!

In that understandable but mistaken belief lie the seeds of postcourtship female shock (the men have their version too).

After the courtship phase of a relationship is over, women often describe their lovers as no longer the verbal, open, caring men they were just a few months back. Many times these women describe their postcourting partners as work-involved, distracted, and generally uninterested in them as people. Not only are women puzzled by this new silent figure in their lives, they often feel tricked, manipulated, and angry. Suddenly, someone you thought was close, on your wavelength, seems to have tuned to another frequency, remote and hard to reach.

Generally, women don't realize that during courtship, unlike during any other time in his life, a man's

54

primary need is to connect emotionally with a future partner and to win her affection and lasting commitment. Often, everything else shifts to second place — work, career, even fatigue. When the intensity of the courtship diminishes, however, when her love and loyalty have been won, most men allow work issues to reappear as their primary concern and their behavior slowly changes to reflect that. Career, success, and achievement reestablish themselves as top priorities. Much to the astonishment of their partners, men's attentive, dashing courtship selves begin to recede into the proverbial past tense.

But it's not men only who take on new and unusual behaviors in the courtship dance. Women have their own parallel set. During courtship, women are more likely to become involved with their lovers' sport activities and hobbies, prepare special meals, plan romantic occasions, write love notes, pay particular attention to how they look, and give lots of luxurious time and attention to their man, to the exclusion of friends, family, and work activities. Women normally involved in demanding career paths will pull back from extra assignments, overtime, and working on weekends. They will downplay their investment in work, put him first, and overly praise him when he joins her in cleaning up after dinner.

Women are likely to be much more sexually active at this time not only because of the excitement and newness of the relationship, but because of the extraordinary attention and emotional outpouring coming from their partners in courtship. A woman is likely to invite sexual overtures, agree readily to nontraditional variations, and even suggest a few of her own.

For men, courtship is a *temporary* aberration in their lives when the love relationship takes priority over all else. Life goes back to normal afterward, or at least what has always been normal for men. The relationship flips into second place and the career back up to first. *But* men expect to remain primary in the lives of their women.

For women, courtship is just the beginning of a *permanent* prioritization of the love relationship, on both sides. After they start living together or after they marry, women expect the relationship to stay Number One.

Women are horrified to find their partners not expecting the same. Men are somewhat horrified, today, to find that they're not exactly the center of their partners' universe.

Starting to Negotiate

The halcyon, or nearly halcyon days of courting beg for perspective. Sometimes a couple comes up against a clash of expectations early on, especially these days, and this is probably a blessing in the end, a tonic for the health and long life of the relationship.

Take the case of Karen and Bill, a couple who had been together for just under a year. Karen is a twenty-eight-year-old accountant, a bright, competent, attractive young professional who came to see me one day because of concerns she was having about the direction, or lack of direction, her present relationship was heading in.

> KAREN: Bill and I have been going together for more than ten months now and I'm getting impatient. I don't feel that I *have* to get married. But I don't really want to be alone either, and I do want to have a family. Mind you, I love Bill, but he doesn't want to make a commitment beyond asking me to move in with him. Frankly, that doesn't

mean much. We spend almost every night now at his place or mine, so living together is no big deal.

I'm also confused about what he really expects. With our friends, he sounds so liberal, like he believes in a fifty-fifty relationship. But with me, even though he's supportive of my career, he always talks about his mother having been there when his dad came home from work and things like that.

He likes to spend a lot of time together, which is all right with me for now. But I've been doing less at work and am beginning to worry about what will happen there for me if things don't work out with Bill.

The major thing that bothers me is his uncertainty. I know he's still recovering from his first marriage and a difficult divorce. When the idea of marriage between *us* comes up, he makes vague references to a prenuptial agreement but then won't pursue it when I am ready to go ahead and talk about it. He's so wishy-washy about all this. If he doesn't want to get married, let him just say so. If he can't make up his mind, I'm ready to forget it!

Now, let's hear from Bill, an up-and-coming investment banker in his early thirties, married once before and now divorced. Karen was his first serious relationship after a number of years of dating around. He was unusually open in his first meeting with me alone.

BILL: I'm not sure what I want. First of all, getting married again feels risky. While I got out of my first marriage without being wiped out financially, I'm certainly going to want some kind of prenuptial contract if I ever marry again, no matter *who* I marry, as unromantic as that sounds.

Things with Karen are moving too fast for me.

She seems ready to get married now, but I find her deadlines a lot of pressure. I guess I'm not sure we're on the same wavelength about what we both want.

I'm interested in having a *wife* and she keeps talking about being my *partner*. Not that I'm against women's lib or anything, but there are lots of things to consider. She's a very loving woman, now. But I wonder how long that will last. Her work is so important to her that it scares me. I think it's great too, but within limits. Whenever I begin to talk about what a great wife my mother was to my dad, in spite of the fact that she worked, Karen doesn't look too happy.

I really don't know what to do.

Bill and Karen are in a fairly typical contemporary courtship dilemma. (Notice that he's worried about *her* work having a priority over him.) Each cares for the other, neither wants the relationship to end, but there are also some very special problems.

First, *timing*. Karen is ready. Bill is not. Karen is feeling the pressure of approaching thirty and knows her pool of potential partners decreases as she gets older. So does her time for childbearing. In her mind, the ten months they have been going together seems like "enough time." They both acknowledge loving one another. They're sexually compatible. They really have a fun time together. Why wait?

For Bill, ten months seems like a short time. He's been married once and feels cautious, not eager. Karen's pressure seems to him inappropriate. It's not that he is looking for someone other than Karen, but he'd like to feel less pursued. He's just not ready.

Timing like this wouldn't have been much of an issue

years back. Most women married early and never had to face today's biological clock. Social norms and men set the pace. Women conformed to that. There was no precedent for a woman to choose the right time to marry, from her point of view. If she wanted to wait, she risked spinsterhood. If she wanted to speed things up, well, about the only way to do that was to get pregnant. But that was a dangerous, uncertain game to play.

Second, *expectations about equality*. Bill and Karen haven't really talked about what each expects of the other in marriage. They are in the middle of a courtship, trying to minimize conflict and to meet each other's needs. Karen has some very firm ideas about having an equal, reciprocal relationship. Bill is much less comfortable with the idea, but doesn't quite know how to say it without sounding like a chauvinist.

During the fifties, how men and women behaved in marriage was much more cut and dried. Everybody knew his or her separate roles. Today, there are real uncertainties about roles. Most women are expecting different things, of themselves and men — they do not want or expect to emulate their parents. Many men are expecting the *same* things — that they will behave like their fathers and their women like their mothers.

Finally, the issue of *nurturing*.

Bill and Karen are at a relatively early stage in their relationship. Neither has children, both are healthy, both are working in jobs they enjoy. Their combined incomes allow them to live quite comfortably. There is no pressure, so each gives freely to the other.

But, remember, this is courtship. Bill is basically a traditional man, even though he's only thirty-two, who wants to be taken care of. ("I'm interested in having a *wife* and she keeps talking about being my *partner*.") He hadn't expressed this much to Karen because she had been meeting his needs just fine.

Karen is a giving woman, but still she is going out of her way now to think of Bill. She doesn't expect to be the only giver in the relationship. She has loved Bill's attentiveness and expects that it will continue.

Given this particular set of circumstances, what could I suggest to Bill and Karen that would help them get through their impasse? Should I recommend to Bill that he move forward, even with his doubts? Should I encourage Karen to move on, even with no guarantees of finding a new man?

I asked Bill and Karen to come to several sessions together. They spent some time talking about the issues. Finally, I made the following suggestion. After determining that neither Bill nor Karen had any religious, family, personal, or business-related objections to living together without being married, I proposed they try it for a three-month period while deciding whether or not to get married. This would provide them with a more accurate reality check for what being married to each other might actually be like.

Whoever joined the other was asked to keep his or her own apartment. This would assure each that they could still maintain a certain sense of independence and that "their place" would be available to go back to in case they decided to break up.

By putting a three-month limit on this experiment, Karen was reassured that they would not drift forever. By putting things on hold for a few months, the pressure was off Bill.

The primary task was to begin talking and acting more like they thought they would in the future. I recommended they both be more frank about what each wanted and expected from the other as marriage partners.

The outcome? Bill and Karen continued living together for almost a year after they began their trial run. They went through a period when Bill was warming up to the idea of getting married and Karen was pulling back. (The pendulum commonly swings like this.) Bill took his turn as pursuer. Karen was having to deal with the major adjustments she'd have to make if she married Bill, both in terms of how much she would have *to give* to the relationship (he expected a lot of her attention) and how much actual support she could expect *to receive* from Bill, particularly in terms of her career aspirations.

Eventually, a balance was reached. They did marry and seem to be doing well. Bill continues to be responsive to Karen's attentions and is increasingly enthusiastic about her work. They are planning to have a child and wondering whether this will change things significantly. I have assured them that it will and sent them off with reading material on parenting.

Men nearing middle adulthood, like Bill, and men riding the crest of a promising career, also like Bill, pose a serious challenge to the women in their lives. These men know that if they are going to "make it," they are going to have to make it by age forty. That's eased up some, but not that much. This places certain traditional stresses on relationship.

These guys are pleased that there is less need now to rush into marriage. It's a big relief. (Compared with the old days, the pressure Bill felt from Karen was mild.) They say that women seem less involved in trying to trap them into marriage, for security or financial reasons. Many welcome the opportunity to date self-sufficient, economically independent women, women who seem to be more up-front about what they need and want.

But when it comes to the woman they are courting, most men are put off by the possibility that her work will become as important to her as his work is to him.

He is in the midst of competing for promotions and fighting like crazy to establish himself in the work world. (Of course, she may be too, and that's the problem.) It is during this time that men can be most demanding, more likely to take than to give and more likely to be narcissistic, inconsiderate, and at times selfish. It is often a time when men become noncommunicative, yet want at the same time to feel cared for and cared about.

So even though a courting man will *say* he's supportive of his lover's career and *appear* understanding when she falls into bed at nine o'clock exhausted by a hard day's work, underneath he's more than likely hoping that her career won't affect his, or his life very much. What he may feel, but never say, is that he'd like her to be home when he gets there.

If He Cares . . .

Meanwhile, women are running their own tests of caring on men, the kind of tests that men find out about only after they've failed. They go something like this.

If he cares, he'll see how tired I am and say, "Let's go out to dinner" even though I offered to cook.

If he cares, he won't ask me to make love tonight because I've got a cold coming on and feel rotten.

If he cares, he'll suggest we have my parents over for brunch on Sunday.

If he cares, he'll encourage me to go to the conference this weekend so I won't feel guilty about leaving.

If he cares, he'll do the dishes without my asking.

Come up against anything resembling these lately? In yourself or in the woman you're living with?

These are just variations of a common internal dialogue that seems unique to women, and not only during the courtship phase. The general formula links certain behaviors with proofs of caring. These become silent tests and unspoken expectations. (This is one area where women are the quintessentially quiet ones.) Sometimes a woman isn't even aware that she is testing. But somehow, in cryptic fashion, she concludes that unless a man acts a certain way, he doesn't care, or care enough.

Men are doubly baffled by this.

First, they talk about how often they feel they're being tested by women, but how distressingly elusive the tests themselves are. (How can you pass when you don't know the questions?)

Secondly, men are notoriously behind women when it comes to caregiving anyway. So even though men know that the general nature of the tests has to do with indications of caring, even their best instincts may fall short, at least in the beginning.

By and large, men have little schooling in the science and art of nurturing. In many ways, they have been actively discouraged from entering this traditionally female domain. So at this particular moment in time, in the area of expressive caring, a real behavioral vacuum yawns between what men are actually delivering and what women are expecting and wanting from them. This poses problems for couples like Karen and Bill. It can even precipitate premature ends to basically good relationships. The next couple were a near miss.

Cindy is thirty-three years old, a successful assistant editor for a major newspaper. She is energetic, outgoing, and accomplished. For a variety of reasons she has not married, although she says she would like to. In a recent therapy session, she told me about the current man in her life. Things had been going well since they began dating about six months earlier. But now she was feeling disenchanted.

CINDY: Hal knew I had to have surgery. It was not a big deal in the sense of being dangerous or life-threatening, but I was frightened anyway. Almost ten years ago, I'd injured my knee while skiing and it had never really healed properly. In fact, it had gotten worse over the years. Surgery was recommended, not the new kind of knee surgery that's done while you're awake, but the heavy-duty stuff — a general anesthetic and a lot of physical therapy afterward, the works. Also, I was going to have to be in the hospital for at least a week after the surgery.

Hal knew all this. And he was very supportive, at first. He even came to the hospital the night I checked in. But after that, I was there for *ten days* and he only came to see me three, maybe four, times. He sent flowers. But that was it!

I mean, I thought we had something going but he really let me down. Believe me, if *he* had been in the hospital, I wouldn't have just visited a gentlemanly few times and sent flowers. I would have been there every day. That's what commitment and caring are all about.

This just might mean the end of our relationship.

To understand Cindy's situation better, I asked Hal to come in and talk with me. Hal was a thirty-eight-year-old electrical engineer who had never talked with a psychologist before and was very uncomfortable about coming. Over the phone, I explained that I wanted to talk with him about his relationship and that he was committing himself for only one meeting. He finally agreed.

HAL: I care for Cindy *a lot*. She's a very special woman and we've been talking about living together — maybe even getting married.

I still don't understand why she got so bent out of shape at me about the surgery. It wasn't like she was seriously ill. She was just going to have her knee taken care of. I knew that Cindy is kind of spooked about doctors and hospitals and all that, so I figured I would go the extra mile. I took her to the hospital the night before and stayed with her until almost ten o'clock that night. The next day I sent flowers. I went to see her several times and I called her every day. She seemed really appreciative the first few days, but then she began to get a little frosty. I mean, everything went all right. She was getting physical therapy during one of my visits when her doctor popped his head into the room to tell her how well she was doing.

Ever since Cindy got out of the hospital there's been a wall between us. I figured that I had done something wrong, but I sure as hell couldn't and still can't figure out what it was. What did she really want from me? To move into the room with her? I've got a demanding job and a lot of responsibilities. I think she expected me to put all those aside because she had this damned operation.

Cindy, as many women would do in the same case, interpreted Hal's behavior in terms of what that behavior would mean if *she* did it. Remember, women will often be much more nurturing than men. If Hal had been in the hospital, Cindy no doubt would have been there every single day, probably more than once. Moreover, when they first began going out, Hal had seemed extraordinarily attentive. However, after they both agreed not to date anyone else, things had begun to change. Hal spent more time at work, seemed less interested in her, and so what occurred in the hospital seemed a further confirmation of his lack of caring.

However, what Hal did was to be there with Cindy during those times that he thought it was *important* — the night before the surgery and the first few days of recovery. He visited, sent flowers, called, and felt that he was available. But, as many other men would, he continued to work and did not significantly alter his life during Cindy's convalescence. Of course, Hal didn't know at all what Cindy expected. So he was confused by her pulling back, her coldness and anger.

To understand better what had occurred around the surgery, Hal and Cindy came together to her next session with me. I asked Cindy to begin by talking about how she felt before and after the surgery. I also asked her to describe what she had wanted from Hal.

Looking first at me and then at Hal, Cindy said, "I was really terrified. The most frightening thing was the anesthetic, but I was ashamed to tell you about it because you kept talking about 'my little operation.' It was great when you came the first night and it really helped. But afterward I felt deserted. You were only there three times!

"I was in a lot of pain. I couldn't even read and I was trying not to take any pain medication. The physical therapy hurt. Whenever I began to talk with you about it, you seemed distracted and uncomfortable.

"I felt abandoned!"

I then asked Hal to tell Cindy how he had felt about her surgery. He said, "First of all, I'm surprised you were that scared. You hadn't said much about it. I

66

didn't think much about the anesthetic being a big deal. I've had three operations and I've always had a general anesthetic.

"Cindy, who the hell knew what was going on in your mind? I figured I was going to get a medal for being 'Mr. Attentive.' If I had known you wanted me to be there every day, I would have been there every day. I mean, why did you keep it such a secret?"

Cindy flushed a bit and then said, "If I have to tell you to visit me every day, it's not the same thing. I really wanted you to come because you *wanted* to be there."

Certainly it is true that Hal could have been more attentive to Cindy during her illness. Daily visits would have been appreciated by her and would not have been inappropriate at all. Hal didn't think his behavior was uncaring. But it was certainly less than what Cindy wanted and expected.

A woman sets herself up for disaster by wishing that a man will intuitively know what she wants or needs, by hoping that he will be aware of her fears or apprehensions, without her expressing these. Because most of the adult men out there these days have not been brought up to be nurturing, women are far more likely to get what they want by *asking* rather than by *hoping*.

I said to Cindy and Hal, "I don't think there are any rights or wrongs in this situation. However, had we not talked, it's likely you would have gotten into worse trouble. Maybe even end what appears to be a pretty good relationship."

They both nodded. I went on: "In terms of the future, let me suggest this. Cindy, you simply have to let Hal know more clearly what you want. If you don't, you're going to continue to feel frustrated and angry and upset.

"Yours is still a relatively new relationship, and while I think Hal can probably anticipate some things as he gets to know you better, for now you're going to have to risk more by asking more. Obviously, one of the consequences is that if you ask and Hal doesn't come through, you're going to be disappointed, and hurt too. But in the end you're going to have a better chance of getting what you want if you ask for it."

Cindy nodded.

"Hal, while I'm asking Cindy to make some changes, I'm not forgetting you. You knew that Cindy was scared. But I think you chose to ignore that. Maybe you feel uncomfortable taking care of Cindy or maybe you just didn't want to take any more time off from work."

Hal was noncommittal.

"I suggest you focus a bit more on Cindy. It does become tiresome if you have to tell somebody *every-thing* you want. One thing you can do is ask questions. Ask Cindy what she wants, what she would like, what she needs."

Hal looked a little hesitant.

"Look, it doesn't mean that every time she says she wants something of you, you have to do it. You have a right to say yes or no, but you're going to be in a better position to make choices if you know more about what Cindy wants from you."

This is not as much of a problem for men, since women are more likely to be spontaneously nurturing. However, the recommendation holds for both sexes; needs are more likely to be met when they are expressed rather than by depending on a partner's mind-reading skills.

Courtship is a wonderful time, and it is also a wonderful training ground, if you let it be. Creative solutions are always, or almost always, possible. For both halves of a couple, the key ingredient, aside from love and chemistry, of course, is the willingness to seek these solutions. Seldom do they appear on their own.

And if what you want is intimacy, it is best to begin now investing yourself in discovering your lover's needs, desires, and dreams, and expressing yours. You'll need all of this to fortify yourself for the journey from courting to the next stage of marrying or living together, long term. This is a major transition. Invest sufficient energy to know what your partner needs, wants, and likes. It is more likely during courtship, but if it doesn't continue, the relationship can end prematurely.

V

Modern Love: Intimacy

Acquiring a *sex life* these days is hardly difficult, either for women or for men. Having a *love life*, or a love life that endures, is less easy to come by. Many of us find that out during our courting days. And if we make it past courting to marriage, marriage of the official or unofficial kind, *all* of us discover this. No one ever told us that getting close, and staying close, could be this hard. No one ever explained that developing intimacy with another person is a process, an uneven one and, if you're lucky, a lifelong one.

Meet Amy and Bob, living together for six years and married for the last three.

Bob is a thirty-five-year-old trim-bearded stockbroker who was clearly troubled when he recounted to me some of the changes that had taken place in his relationship with Amy. This is Amy's first marriage, Bob's second, and they have an eighteen-month-old son.

One of the main reasons Bob's earlier marriage ended was that he and his first wife were never able, even with expert counseling, to feel really close. Their sex life was nearly nonexistent. He thought his problems were over when he met Amy.

Bob began: "During the time we were going together it was absolutely wonderful. Amy was fun, romantic, enthusiastic, and sensual. Sex was great for me, and I assume for you [Bob turned toward Amy, who nodded]. There was even a time last year when we were out for dinner one night and, between coffee and dessert, went out to the car for a quickie. It wasn't always that way, but overall things were pretty terrific."

He looked over at Amy and continued: "Now, everything has changed. Amy is into herself, work, and the baby. We rarely make love. I mean [to Amy], if the baby makes a sound, or if you've got a meeting the next morning, or if you're tired, or if *anything,* you just don't seem very interested. Oh, sure, sometimes you'll go along. But Amy, I have a feeling you're not really there."

Amy is thirty and, in addition to first-time motherhood, works part-time as a paralegal in a law office nearby. A slender, attractive woman who wears comfortable cottons and simple wire-rimmed glasses, she responded quietly: "Bob is right about how things were when in the beginning. But many things *were* different then. We didn't have a baby. We were living separately. And when we were together, it was just the two of us. I wasn't trying to juggle so many things."

She sounded sad as she continued: "Besides, *then* Bob was the most attentive, caring, loving man I had ever met. He would talk for hours. I knew that sex was really important to him. It was and still is very nice for me. But it is true that whether or not we make love is not as critical to me now. And if I'm tired or if there are things needing doing, I sometimes can't get into it."

Amy paused as if to catch her breath and her thoughts. Then: "Bob hardly talks to me anymore. He comes home, helps with dinner, and then reads or watches television. If I ask him about work, he gets a pained expression on his face and usually responds with 'It's fine.' He doesn't talk about his world and he never asks me about mine.

"Sometimes, what I'd like is for Bob to sit next to me and hold me. I mean [her voice rose], I feel close that way, warm and loving just being with him, being held, his arm around me. I don't understand why it can't be the same for Bob."

I spent some time alone with Bob and asked him to reflect upon how he might have changed since he and Amy married and how this might be affecting her. He acknowledged that he was working harder, getting home after seven several nights a week, and putting in Saturday mornings at the office. He said he didn't often call Amy during the day and that they had not been out for an evening alone in more than three months.

"I guess I'm not around home nearly as much. And when I am, I spend a lot more time by myself. Amy's right. I don't talk to her very much, at least not nearly as much as I used to. I've just been more into myself. And I have been really angry with her about how different she seems and that we don't make love very often. When things get to me, I either close up or blow up and that doesn't help either."

I pointed out to Bob that Amy was not necessarily being rejecting, but that she was somewhat, if not a lot, overwhelmed with all the competing pressures of home, work, and mothering. I also reminded him that for most women and probably for Amy, feeling closely connected to their mate was part of, and often a pre-requisite for, feeling sexually loving.

To help him begin changing things, I suggested to Bob that he organize one night out alone with Amy, just the two of them, every week. I also suggested that Bob let Amy know earlier in the evening when he felt like making love. Then if Amy felt particularly wiped out or distracted, she could either let Bob know that or refocus on him.

Bob proposed the weekly night out idea to Amy and she was delighted. She began opening up to Bob about how much she had missed their talking *and* how exhausted she sometimes felt. Things slowly got back on track for them.

Intimate Differences

This couple had found themselves tangled in the kind of cross-purposes that tend to reveal themselves in the middle and later stages of relationships. Remember the earlier tangles we talked about with respect to the differences in how the sexes approach sex and commitment? Well, once the commitment issue is put to rest, once a relationship deepens, these tend to modulate into sex and intimacy differences.

Let's take another look at Bob and Amy's situation. It was pointed out that, for Amy, a sense of intimacy was not necessarily tied to lovemaking. It might *lead* to lovemaking, but being held and being together could be very satisfying, in and of themselves, to Amy as to most women.

What about Bob?

How men approach intimacy is a less commonly understood and little talked about phenomenon. For most men, men like Bob, intimacy and sex are inex-

73

tricably linked. That's not to say that men can't be sexual without being intimate. (Men, in fact, are quite good at doing that, as mentioned earlier.) But it's exceedingly hard for men to be intimate without being sexual. Lovemaking usually needs to *precede* any feeling of closeness with women. Sexuality is the base of their coming together, emotionally, with women.

What another contrary we have here! Because, of course, the reverse is generally true for women — intimate feelings usually need to come before sex, or good sex anyway. There are just more of them afterward.

Men have begun to understand the woman's side of this largely because women have told us about it. But women are trailing behind in understanding the male side, as I believe men are themselves.

I tried to explain all this to Amy after she frustratedly talked to me in a later session about how much less verbal Bob had become. I told her how men are often more open, expressive, and intimate as a result of making love. (Remember, she and Bob hadn't been doing much of that.) This seemed to strike a chord.

She said, "That's absolutely true! Bob is often much more talkative after we make love. But until you pointed it out, I never connected the two. Now that I think about it, this was true even when we were going together. We'd often go to bed first, then get up and cook dinner, and talk for hours."

Amy then smiled. "Then, lots of times we'd go back and make love again. It was wonderful!"

There are several other related issues of intimacy for men that most women don't understand, or understand only dimly.

- Most men have only *one* person with whom they are intimate — their wife or their lover, *not* their male buddies, as is commonly believed. This leaves men

74

extraordinarily vulnerable and dependent upon their wives or living-together partners.

- Because of this, most men experience their partners' lack or lessening of time and attention as rejection, abandonment, significant loss, or some combination of these. This usually gets expressed as anger. *"Where the hell were you until seven o'clock!"* might mean *"I missed you and was worried."*
- For the many reasons already given, most men are far less emotionally expressive than women, with the exception of generalized anger, that is. They don't do well when it comes to talking about relationship issues.

Most couples eventually run into trouble with all of the above — especially now that women have as many, if not more, demands on their time and pulls on their attention.

"What about Me?"

Jeff and Sandy had been married for nearly twenty years when I first met them. Jeff had recently been promoted to assistant manager for a supermarket after having worked his way up from the ranks of stock clerk and checker. He was taking in-service courses and was excited about his new responsibilities and job. Sandy had an equally successful full-time job in computer sales. They had two children, ages fourteen and seventeen.

Jeff began: "I don't understand why it's so difficult to get through to Sandy. There are so many things going on in my life right now. My days are just filled. When I get home at the end of the day, wanting to talk with Sandy about it, to tell her what's been going on, she keeps putting me off. First we have to eat dinner, then the kids need something, or a friend calls. Then she has to do an hour or so of paperwork. By the time she's ready to talk I forgot what it was I wanted to talk to her about."

Sandy responded: "Jeff is really unrealistic. When he comes home, everyone is dying to eat. After dinner, the children need time to talk, and the only chance I get to do my sales reports is in the evening. He's the one who's encouraged me to continue working, yet he's always complaining that I'm not available."

Jeff now turned to me and said slowly and sadly: "You know, Sandy seems to be surrounded. She talks with her sisters, her girlfriends, even with her mother, but she's the only one that *I* really have. If I can't talk with her, I've got no one else. I feel abandoned."

His voice began to rise. "I've told Sandy how *angry* I am — that she is being selfish, and that I am tired of being taken for granted."

Jeff told *me* he felt abandoned. He told *Sandy* he was angry. Most men have difficulty identifying, acknowledging, and certainly sharing feelings of loneliness and hurt. They tend to become angry instead. What the anger tends to do in turn is drive people away. This is precisely what was happening to Jeff.

Sandy was continually being criticized and was beginning to feel irritated herself. She was doing the best she could — working, parenting, and still attempting to be a wife, friend, and lover to Jeff. His insistence on her full attention seemed unreasonable and self-indulgent.

Because Jeff and Sandy's situation was so critical, I spent time with Jeff alone. I found out that Jeff is a quiet man who has few friends and who doesn't ordinarily talk a lot. Sandy is truly the only person he confides in. It was important for Sandy to understand that Jeff wasn't being unreasonable, but that he really needed her to be there for him.

Jeff knew that Sandy was not trying to ignore him. He knew intellectually that the ends of her days were filled with work, friends, and family. He knew that she maintained their social calendar. Yet emotionally he felt there was no place for him.

We came up with a rather simple solution that met both Jeff's needs for time and Sandy's sense of responsibility to others. The first half hour after Jeff's arrival home from work was "theirs." They would move into the den, sometimes have a drink, put on the answering machine, and just talk. Then the evening's other activities would commence. Dinner was put back only a half hour, but it was well worth it.

The Myth of Male Bonding

Most women have multiple outlets for emotional support. They are likely to have a close personal network of friends and family, people they can really talk to, especially other women. So it often comes as a surprise to them that most men don't have these kinds of intimate relations, not even men who spend time with other men.

This is not much of a surprise to men, who know that while they may spend time sharing *activities* with other men, they rarely spend time sharing *themselves*.

Many women will say that when they first meet a woman, at a business lunch, for instance, the initial forty-five minutes are spent getting to know each other, the last fifteen minutes are spent on business. For men, the same circumstances go quite differently. If they do talk personally before the actual business talk begins, they will share biographical information — where they went to school, where they worked before, their current role or position, perhaps if they're married and have children — but rarely more than that and only briefly. They then move immediately into a business discussion.

Would men talk about things that they're frightened about, excited about, or confused about with a male colleague or acquaintance? Not on your life! The only person they're likely to share these thoughts with is the woman in their life. A client of mine, Don, a forty-five-year-old manufacturing rep, tells this story about himself and a friend of his: "Paul and I have been running together for, I guess, oh hell, maybe a year, twice a week. We go about five or six miles, usually at a good pace. But this one Sunday we began pushing each other and by the time it was over we were both out of breath and almost gasping. I told him he looked wiped out. He nodded his head and said, 'Yeah, I've been wiped out a lot this year.' "

Paul then proceeded to tell Don that for the past year he'd been under severe financial strain, had made some bad investments, and almost gone bankrupt. Don, my client, then told Paul about the anxiety attacks he'd been having, the fact that he was in therapy, and that he was also having some marital problems.

Both Don and Paul talked about how strange it was that they had been running together for a year and had never talked about any of these problems. Paul said: "Let's agree that if either of us gets into trouble over the next year, we ask the other for help. Okay?"

Don said he agreed. As our session drew to an end, I turned to him and asked whether he thought either he or Paul would actually do it. Don smiled at me, shook his head, and said, "No way."

The truth is that men will rarely, if ever, share intimate feelings with other men, especially intimate *sad* feelings. It is for this reason that men often seem to be making inordinate demands for time with the women in their lives and particularly time alone. As Mike, a thirty-seven-year-old draftsman, said about his wife: "Somehow I can't get across to her that when I want to spend time with her, I just want to spend time with her — not with her and the kids, not with her and another couple, just with *her*. There is nobody else I talk to. So if she's not there, it's just me alone."

Leslie, a fashion consultant in her early forties, wrote the following letter about her husband six months after having heard me speak on the subject of men's limited outlets for intimacy:

It's been absolutely fascinating. Fred and I have always had a good marriage. In fact, I would call it better than good. Because of that I had taken things somewhat for granted. He was always suggesting that we go out for breakfast together without the kids, or go out for a glass of wine in the evening. Frankly, I hadn't paid much attention to him. Sometimes I'd say yes. It depended on what was going on in my life. You know, it's hard trying to juggle work, kids, and a husband too. But I'd noticed that Fred seemed to be getting a bit more distant. Sex had become less frequent and less intense.

Just as an experiment, I began to pay more attention to Fred. When he said he wanted to spend time alone with me, I said yes. I either responded immediately or told him specifically why I couldn't and then set up a time for us to be together.

Things have changed! I thought our relationship was good before, but now it's absolutely spectacular. Fred is much less resentful about the time I spend at work — even about my trips. He seems to be much more understanding. When I do get home late, he's there and doing things like emptying the dishwasher. That was unheard of for Fred! Probably, though, the best thing of all has been the change when we make love. It's unbelievably special. One of the things I try to do is make sure there's enough time so that it's not a rush-rush experience. I think I'm getting more out of it than he is!

Switching Course Midstream

It's one thing to have married a working woman only to discover within yourself later the desire to have more of her time. It's another to have been in a more or less traditional marriage, yourself the breadwinner, your wife the homemaker, and then suddenly, once the nest empties, the woman you could always count on to be there decides to enter, or reenter, the workplace.

This is happening to midlife couples all the time today. Midlife men are thrown by this, and often their partners have little awareness of the impact their changing course is having.

Take the case of Sam and Judy.

Sam is a forty-six-year-old building contractor who has been married to Judy for twenty-three years. Judy recently completed a certificate program in computer programming and now has her first full-time job since she stopped teaching school some eighteen years ago. Sam was pleased that Judy was going back to work. He knew she was bright and, at the age of forty-five, with children no longer at home, she needed to be doing something new with her life. He gave her a lot of support during her training program and was pleased when she began her new job. Now, however, he is feeling different.

SAM: I think if I had known what was going to happen I might not have been as gung-ho for Judy to go back to work. I feel caught. I know that Judy is pushing hard and I know work takes a lot out of her. But I feel *we're* drifting apart.

Frankly, it's not work that's getting in the way.

It's the way she treats me. I seem to be pretty far down on her list of priorities. First, it's her job. Then it's talking with the kids. Then it's her friends. Then it's calling her parents. Then, I guess, it's me.

Last night we were going to be together and had actually finished dinner and the dishes early. It was probably no more than seven or seven thirty when we went into the family room. We hadn't made love for weeks. I had some wine poured and had put on some music. Just as we sat down, the phone rang. It was one of her friends who had some kind of problem. So she went into the other room and talked with her friend for — I timed it — forty-five minutes! She came back in, yawning, and said, "Where were we?"

When I told her how angry I was that she let her girlfriend's problems be more important than our being together, she blew up and told me that I was selfish and inconsiderate. Obviously we didn't make love that night either.

Judy is the one who tells me how sensitive *she* is, how aware *she* is, how much *she* knows about relationships. Well, that may be true. But, in terms of us, she doesn't have any idea what the hell is going on.

I'm not sure how to approach her because she seems irritated about something half the time. I really thought that as women began to work and feel better about themselves, their relationships were supposed to get better. Well, let me tell you, it's not happening.

One major threat to long-term relationships occurs when a woman's involvement with family, career, children, friends leads her to be unavailable, uninterested, or unappreciative of the intimate and sexual needs of the man in her life. Men need to feel like a priority in their partners' life and to have that expressed in words and actions.

Many men are dismayed by the lack of time for love-making. They describe their "changing" partners as always tired, and seemingly distracted. Many men complain that they get her time when everything and everybody else has been taken care of.

Many of today's middle-aged men don't believe that the changes in women's lives are at all good for them. They often wonder if it's worth it when wives leave home at seven thirty in the morning, return home at seven, yawn by eight, and are asleep by nine.

For Sam, the first twenty years of marriage were very comfortable. Judy was attentive, available, and affectionate. She really seemed to care about him. However, now she has other things that she's excited about. Going back to work has been a very positive experience for her. In the midst of all that, she still maintains all the relationships she previously had — with her children, her parents, and her many friends. Interestingly enough, Judy views Sam's requests for her time as somehow a burden, not an invitation.

Sam contributes to the problem by expressing the usual male anger rather than telling her what he really feels is loneliness. When we talked in therapy, he was able to express greater feelings of vulnerability. But he has more difficulty doing this with Judy. Most often what he does with her is complain.

Like the other men we've discussed, Sam doesn't have the network of friendships that Judy has, so Judy's unavailability leads him to feel particularly empty. Also, Sam is a fairly conservative man. He doesn't have "outside" relationships, so Judy's decreased interest in sex because of fatigue is a real source of frustration to him.

As a result of working with Sam and Judy, the following solutions emerged:

- Sam agreed to begin telling Judy when he was feeling lonely rather than just acting angry.
- Judy agreed that she could probably not continue to be the emotional shoulder for many of her women friends if she intended to have time to devote to Sam. She became less available to them, more available to him.
- Both acknowledged that their lives were more complex now than they were before and they could not depend upon times emerging spontaneously for them to be together, both intimately and sexually. They'd have to do more planning.

Some two years later, things with Judy and Sam were going well. Her work had become less demanding and she was spending less evening time on projects. Sam had developed several male friends and was out with them once or twice a week. Sex was more frequent and more satisfying to both of them since she wasn't as tired and he wasn't as frustrated.

In working with men and women on these issues it has become clear that *time* is the lubricant of relationships and without it all relationships will eventually grind to a halt. Yet time alone is the one thing that couples are least likely to give themselves. They get what's left over, after all the tasks are completed.

What a couple needs minimally if a relationship is to endure is:

1. *Time to talk.* This should be twice weekly at least, and not after nine at night, when all disagreements

bypass the argument stage and become instant disasters.

2. *Time to play.* Many men and women have forgotten what it's like to have fun, to share activities that they both enjoy.

3. *Time to make love.* Often couples recall how they were at the beginning of their relationship: making love just seemed to happen. Spontaneity is wonderful when it works, but often, with the complicated lives men and women live, it doesn't. Planning ahead ("let's get together tonight") may sound like work, but it's likely to be effective.

So now, having made this journey with me from the chaos of first meetings through the dance of courtship to the bittersweet of intimacy, what have you learned? First, and perhaps foremost, that relationships are difficult and need constant work. Second, that our rapidly changing world has added even more turbulence to this river of emotion. Third, that you need to both persevere *and* adapt if you are to survive.

So if you are single and having a hard time trying to figure out what he or she really wants; if you're at the courting stage and things seem so incredibly complicated; or if you have made it to intimacy and feel overwhelmed by the demands it engenders, you're probably dealing with the usual and normal problems associated with finding and forming a relationship.

VI

If She's Out Hunting Tigers,
Why Won't He
Clean Up the Hut?

I wasn't going to include a chapter about housework in this book. After all, is there anything in the world that is inherently less interesting to a man than *housework*? I mean, who cares! Just get the damn stuff done as quickly as possible, preferably by somebody else. This is a book about men, and real men don't talk (or write) about housework.

So why did I change my mind? Because, the one question that is asked of me most often by women, after a talk, in therapy, or even in social situations, is, "How can I get my husband, partner, or boyfriend to do more at home?" While this question is more usual from women who work full-time, it is also asked by those who go to school, work part-time, have significant volunteer commitments, or are planning to reenter the work force. Of all the things I talk about to audiences of men and women, this is the one topic that is most likely to lead men and women into angry yelling matches. Each seems to have no awareness of why the other person feels so different.

Arguments about housework are the leading cause of domestic violence in the United States. This is an area where men and women seem to have no common basis of understanding. Even the same words, like "helping out," have a different meaning depending upon your gender. For men, "helping out" is a positive statement, an offer of support, and a willingness to participate. For women, "helping out" is heard as a token, as half-hearted, as grudging, since she feels left with the responsibility.

For a woman, saying "I have to get the dishes put away before I can come into the den" is to make a statement of reality, is even her indirect way of saying she's overloaded. For a man, these same words sound like a guilt trip, or another example of her compulsiveness, or simply a matter of screwed-up priorities. He thinks, "We'll get to that tomorrow morning. Leave the damned dishes and get in here with me."

For women, it seems only logical that if they are going to be doing more *outside* the home, men should be willing to do more *inside* the home. It seems reasonable and fair to women that if they have a twenty- or thirty- or forty-hour-per-week job, helping to support the family or couple, housework would automatically become a joint enterprise.

Women become surprised when he doesn't spontaneously pitch in (which is what *they* would do), confused when he gets angry at her for bringing up the topic, and withdraw resentfully when he then needs constant reminding to do what it was he agreed to do. They simply don't understand why men behave as they do, but they desperately want to so that they can both get some relief and stop being so angry!

As said before, just twenty-five years ago there were few working women and certainly no terminology such as "two-career couples." In the sixties men went off to work every morning while women stayed at home. Men earned the family income while women vacuumed, ironed shirts, and did all the things their mothers had taught them to do. That's the way it was. No one really thought much about whether men and women were happy in those separate domains.

Today, the majority of adult American women work outside the home, full-time. If they don't, they are probably going back to school to prepare for a job, working part-time, or thinking about it. Like their husbands, a great many women leave home at seven in the morning, put in a long day's work, and come home as tired as their partners. Yet most women still complete 85 percent of all the tasks involved in maintaining a home, irrespective of the level they have achieved in their jobs or careers. The skills they have gained in the workplace — whether preparing a legal brief, running a meeting, or firing an incompetent employee — have not helped them to overcome their socialization as head of home maintenance. Women still feel a sense of bottom-line responsibility for the home. For them, the home is another workplace.

Women tell me they don't want to feel responsible, but they do. What they keep hoping is that the men in their lives will begin to feel some of the responsibility. Some women would be satisfied if their men would just take up picking up after themselves. They are upset that men haven't and don't feel any responsibility, and probably won't! They can't believe that men are so indifferent to the distress they feel about this unshared area of their shared life together. Many women become angry. That anger is affecting male-female relationships in a way that has implications for us all.

The more I talk with women, the more I realize how upset they are about this housework issue. The more I talk with men, the more I realize how far from reconciliation the sexes are. Men can't believe women could be so angry about something as insignificant as housework. Men think surely the anger must be about something other than this, something much more important. They can't figure out what it could be.

What happens when women get angry? Well, usually they hold it in, and keep it in, until some insignificant event touches off a mini-tirade or emotional explosion. Why do women do this? Because girls were raised to feel that anger is inappropriate, bad under most circumstances. And anger, even when acknowledged, should never be expressed. So women often don't even recognize when they are angry. And if they do, they are loath to acknowledge it. It's not nice for women to get angry.

As a consequence, I find many women silently furious, but denying that anything specific is wrong. Some get depressed. Some have physical symptoms. Others feel immobilized, unable to do anything except lash out at people around them with accusations and condemnations, often not even related to the source of the irritation.

So what do men do when confronted with these depressed, withdrawn, (seemingly) constantly complaining partners? You've got it. *They* get openly angry, often. Anger is a very different emotion for men, as said earlier. Boys in our culture are permitted anger and aggression. In fact, these emotions are encouraged, so that boys don't behave like "sissies." Emotions like hurt, sadness, or fear are discouraged. That's being like a girl (God forbid). In our culture, Father and Mother smile when Johnny protects little sister from the bully, but still say, "See here, young lady," when six-year-old Jane begins to raise her voice.

So we find men and women experiencing anger about housework in very different ways. Women talk openly with one another about this dilemma. But after a few unsuccessful attempts with their partners, they cease talking, withdraw, or sometimes attack. Men are frustrated by partners who seem too often upset, withdrawn, complaining, and occasionally explosive. So the anger dance goes on.

On the man's side of things, intellectually he knows that in order for his family to buy a home, own two cars, go on vacations, and send children to college, it will probably require two incomes. Most men agree that their wives' financial contributions are needed. Men also realize that women thrive on the challenge and stimulation that comes from having a paying job outside the home. They see their partners happier and more productive in general when their opportunities extend beyond housewife and mother. Few men today would argue that a woman's place is in the home. Most are encouraging their wives to work and are proud of their successes (unless, of course, she's *too* successful — more about that later). If anything, there is a new social prejudice today against women who *don't* work outside the home.

Given all this, men *know* that it is unreasonable for women to bear the entire burden for maintaining a home. They *understand* logically that she needs to be supported. They *recognize* that no work is inherently sex-linked (many remember that making a bed and scrubbing the barracks was not considered woman's work in the military).

Yet they *feel* different.

You see, we are in a time warp. For most men, home is a haven, a place to return to, a place to relax, to turn off. Housework is just a peripheral annoyance that somehow has to be dealt with. Men become involved emotionally only when housework isn't done or when they are feeling coerced about it by wives or partners.

Most men (and women) were raised in traditional homes where roles were cut and dried. Except on rare occasions, few men saw their fathers wash dishes, change diapers, mop floors, or clear tables. As young boys, while helping Dad take out the garbage, put up the storm windows, or adjust the television antenna, they saw their mothers and sisters perform the traditionally female chores.

Obviously, these images are truer for older than for younger men today, and they depend somewhat on the personal history each man brings to a relationship. However, many men deep down want "a girl just like the girl who married dear old Dad." But wanting a traditional relationship is not congruent with today's culture. Men are *embarrassed* by these feelings because that's not what they're supposed to be experiencing. They keep them quiet, telling neither wives nor girlfriends and certainly not their male friends.

Most men really do feel that housework is a nuisance. They don't like to do it, and when they do, never feel as good having washed the kitchen floor as having waxed the car. Men don't brag about how much "they help out at home" to other men (or women). Men were raised to be breadwinners, not to vacuum and dust, and even though they are doing more, it is usually without joy. From a socialization standpoint, housework is women's work.

"It's stupid. I should be beyond this. But I just feel

90

uncomfortable making beds — incompetent too. It's not that complicated, but damn it, even when I put in the time, it looks lumpy."

"The one time she put an apron on me, I just exploded. That was too much."

"It infuriates me when she picks up her clothes and leaves mine. I know our deal was that we would each pick up after ourselves, but something doesn't sit right. Damn it, I don't just do *my* income taxes and leave *hers!*"

Actually, men are participating in housework much more and with less reluctance than ever before. However, even when relatively unresistant, men experience a sense of overload similar to women's — the Superman counterpart to the Superwoman syndrome. Men still do what they have always done: work full-time, go to school, or both. Now, on top of that, they cook, make beds, wash dishes, and go shopping for groceries.

However, the men I talk to tell me they feel caught in a role of ever-increasing expectations. They feel continually admonished for what they *don't* do rather than acknowledged for what they *do* do. They also report that housework is not something they do automatically, like checking the oil in the car, but have to think about consciously. So, even men who truly do their fair share rarely have the emotional investment in the household arena that their wives or lovers do. They see themselves as "helping out" rather than feeling ultimately responsible — still.

Here's yet another dimension to all this. You recall that in the last chapter we explored the loss a man may feel when his partner seems unavailable. This has

91

its impact in the household arena too. Many men feel they get the post-housework leftovers of their partner's time and energy. He's upset when she's not willing to relax with him until every last dish is put away. He feels abandoned in the morning when she won't linger in bed for just a few more minutes. He misses the supportive care he thought he'd be getting. But how does he act? What does he say? Does he share his feelings of loneliness? Of course not. He gets mad! Remember, anger is the more available and more acceptable emotion to men. How do women respond when men become angry? Frightened, first. Then withdrawn. How do men respond to this retreat? With more anger.

Look at the results of a recent survey.

Men and women were asked to list in order of importance the problems they each had in dealing with their relationship.

- Money was number one for both.
- For women, housework was number two. (Housework never even appeared on the men's list!)
- For men, loneliness was number two. (Loneliness never even appeared on the women's list!)

So, what is to be done? Back in the early eighties when I first wrote about housework, my solutions were pragmatic: finding ways to divide responsibilities, finding and using help, reevaluating standards of what represents a "clean" house. While these solutions still hold, they are virtually impossible to implement until and unless women understand more about why men feel as they do.

Let's Spend the Morning in Bed

Josh and Eleanor were a newly married couple whom I had been seeing in therapy for about six months. He

92

was thirty-four; she thirty-five, and both had previously been married. They'd been together for more than two years and seemed very compatible. However, they found themselves frequently disagreeing about such things as how to spend a Saturday morning.

Josh, tall, slender, and curly-haired, described a recent argument: "Eleanor and I both work very hard and, by the time we get home at the end of the day, we're beat. I also go to a night class twice a week, so often I just come in, grab some food, and run out. By the time I get home, Eleanor is asleep. She also has to go to her office on Saturdays about twice a month and that really makes things tight for us.

"I look forward to weekends for us to be together. We hardly get any other time."

Josh turned to Eleanor. "Last Saturday was a real opportunity. I didn't have any exams to study for, you didn't have to go to the office, there was nothing on the agenda. It could have been a great day.

"What I had in mind was breakfast, maybe making love, and then spending the afternoon together —"

Eleanor broke in: "But things were such a mess. There were clothes all over the room, newspapers on the floor, laundry from the past week. The place hadn't been vacuumed. The bathroom was awful. All I wanted to do was spend the morning getting things put together so that *I* could relax and then I would be ready to spend the day with you. But when I asked you to help, you threw a fit, and went out on the beach to play volleyball with your buddies. Some togetherness!"

When Eleanor and Josh were dating and discussing their future, she was encouraged by Josh's seemingly comfortable attitude about cooking, cleaning, and other domestic chores. "You can count on me," he said. When they began living together he did pitch in. He generally did the shopping, joined Eleanor with the dishes, washed his clothes, and put the bedroom together before leaving for work.

Still, Eleanor spent more time in cooking, cleaning, and other household chores than Josh did. On *that* Saturday she was looking forward to getting finally caught up. She wanted Josh to help her get the house in order so that she could relax and then enjoy the day. When Josh refused and then left her to go play volleyball, she felt both disappointed and rejected.

Josh was equally upset. Some of his reasons for choosing Eleanor was that she was a warm, loving, and affectionate woman. He liked that. He knew that Eleanor was committed to her career, but there was always time for him.

During the months before they married, she was enthusiastic about his plans and seemed always to be available. He felt hurt that particular Saturday by her unwillingness to be with him and her insistence on spending the day getting the house clean. He didn't really care how things looked. He wanted to be with Eleanor, but not cleaning house.

To understand why Eleanor and Josh are having difficulties, we must recall some of the differences between men and women. Most men have no personal investment in the house and will do housework only because they know that it's the right thing to do. Men's bachelor pads often are chaotic, and most men are not bothered by this. When they marry or begin living with a woman, they are pleased to be in more pleasant surroundings, but certainly do not feel upset when things are not put together perfectly.

Most men today are willing to participate. But the words they use capture their true feelings. "I'll do my part." "I'll help you." "I'll pitch in." They like it when it's neat and clean, but they're not emotionally affected when it's not.

94

Most women identify with their homes and feel physically and psychologically uncomfortable if things are in massive disarray. They feel burdened with the responsibility of the household and both want and expect their partners to do their fair share. They often interpret men's reluctance to participate as noncaring and are upset when direct requests are refused.

When Eleanor wouldn't be available until after the house was cleaned, Josh just couldn't understand "what her problem was." He wanted housecleaning to be deferred until later. He simply couldn't respond to Eleanor's discomfort. Eleanor felt that Josh was acting in a selfish and inconsiderate fashion. She was so upset she didn't want to be with him at all.

What did Josh and Eleanor need to know in order to resolve their impasse?

Josh had to understand that Eleanor was incapable of relaxing as long as their home was chaotic. Eleanor needed to see that Josh was not as affected as she was by the condition of their home and that he was not rejecting her so much as he was her choice of cleanliness over companionship.

By the way, there are certainly times when men feel more strongly about order than women do. However, the same principles hold. If the more responsible or compulsive partner has an assurance that the chaos will be attended to in a reasonable fashion and within a specific time frame, he or she is much more likely to feel relaxed. By the same token, if the partner who has the greater need for spending time together knows that the amount of time devoted to tasks is limited and defined, he or she is much more willing to participate without feeling resentful.

After I had thoroughly discussed the situation with Josh and Eleanor, we began to deal with solutions. We set up some ground rules that seemed to make sense to both. First, there was to be an absolute limit as to the amount of time that would be devoted to household tasks on the weekend. Josh and Eleanor both agreed that two hours would be the maximum to be spent on housecleaning on free days. However, these tasks were a priority. Josh agreed that he would work with Eleanor *before* beginning to get involved in recreational activities. He also agreed to be more positive in his approach. Eleanor agreed to be less aggravated by Josh's casual attitude toward the house. She accepted that he was less likely to respond to clutter by spontaneously straightening things up. She seemed thoughtful as she said: "When things get too uncomfortable for Josh, he's likely to move to another room. It's funny too, because he dresses immaculately, is very well groomed, and makes sure his car is washed every week. But he can walk by a pile of newspapers four or five times and never think of picking them up."

Even though I had had many variants of Josh and Eleanor in my office over the years, I was never truly convinced that women really "identified" with their home. It just didn't make any sense to me (being a man, of course).

It wasn't until I actually saw for myself how powerful an issue this is that I was able to understand it and help other men understand it too.

His Haven, Her Workplace

One last housework drama.

Some years ago I spent an evening with a truly egalitarian couple. Melissa was an articulate, well-respected feminist who had a very successful management consulting business. Frank was in state government. Their children were grown and had left home. They were living comfortably, had enough money, and had work that was meaningful to them. They also shared the housework and used no outside help.

After going out to dinner, I was invited back to their home for coffee. They had just renovated an old house and were anxious to show me through. The tour progressed uneventfully until we got to the bedroom, which proved to be a disaster area (the way most bedrooms look if they haven't been cleaned up). The bed was unmade, pajamas and robes were strewn about, drawers were half open, coffee cups and juice glasses were on the floor. The bathroom door was ajar and disorder reigned there also.

Frank continued to describe enthusiastically what they had done to the house. He pointed out how they had put in a skylight, created workspaces for both, and had changed an unneeded window box into bookshelves. He seemed no different in the messy bedroom than he had been in the spotless living room.

Melissa? She looked flustered and was frantically closing drawers, smoothing the bed, and trying to make the room look presentable. She was also glaring at Frank.

We returned to the living room and had our coffee (which he prepared). At one point in the conversation Melissa talked about how much she valued Frank's sense of fairness and how balanced a life they led as a couple. This seemed to be an excellent opportunity for me to assume my psychologist/researcher role, so I turned to him and said, "Frank, by the way, how did you feel about the fact that the bedroom was a mess just now?"

Frank said, with a puzzled look on his face, "How did I feel about it? Why should anybody have any feelings about something like that? We just hadn't gotten around to it. I guess I didn't feel *anything*. I hadn't even noticed it."

I then turned to Melissa and posed the same question to her. Melissa replied, "It's dumb. It's idiotic. But I felt embarrassed and uncomfortable, like I had been caught! I was somewhat furious with Frank for not having cleaned up this morning. You know, it was your turn!"

Frank shrugged his shoulders and went on to another topic. To him, it was no big deal.

It is not that Frank and Melissa had not seen the same things. I'm certain that Frank could have been as accurate as Melissa in describing the state of the room. It is simply that it affected them differently.

For Melissa, the disarray was an emotionally upsetting experience. She would have felt irritated even had I not been there, but my presence accentuated this feeling. Melissa doesn't want to feel this way, but she does. For Frank, the messy bedroom had no emotional import. It's not that Frank couldn't see the mess, he (and many other men) simply reacts differently from Melissa (and many other women).

What is most difficult for women to accept is that men don't feel the same way they do. Melissa clearly did not believe Frank when he said that the bedroom didn't bother him. But then, later in the evening, he said to Melissa, "It's like you and the car. Remember last week when I saw the scratch on the door and went crazy? You saw the scratch too, but it didn't affect you at all! That's the way the house affects me. I see things but they just don't bother me the same way they do you. I'm not being nasty or insensitive or even passive-aggressive. I'm just not affected the same way!"

Women will be continually upset if they believe that men's behavior is somehow a type of latent chauvinism. Men will be continually irritated if they believe that she's just being bitchy again.

We must continue to look at this issue in a broader context. In the previous chapter I pointed out that men do not have many intimate relationships. When his special woman is not available, a man feels abandoned. This becomes even more difficult when a woman is involved in a more complicated life-style, when she has a career, maintains a full social calendar, and keeps in touch with friends, family, and colleagues. The most difficult thing for a man to accept is his not being a priority.

Women do not understand that what men want most from women is their attention and presence. Men don't express this need very well and women don't seem to "get it" when they do. I was told the following story by a woman who had been working very hard at trying to maintain herself, her job, and her marriage.

I think I finally understood what you had been saying about men wanting to feel connected this past weekend. We were having a dinner party, and I was doing it the smart way. My guests were bringing dessert, the salad was mixed, and the gumbo just had to be heated.

Max was in the den watching a ball game, and I needed to have the tablecloth and napkins ironed. So I set up the ironing board in the den, and asked Max if he would iron them while he watched the game. He seemed surprised, but said okay. I felt great — I was getting the help I needed without getting Max upset. So I went up to the bedroom to read.

Then Max walked in and asked me to come join him in the den. He knows I don't like basketball, but he said: "I don't care whether you watch or read, or even take a nap. I just want to be with you, *and* I want you to want to be with me."

Max had said things like that before, but I never really heard him. One of the things that's different is that I'm not so mad at him all the time, and I guess it has to do with his helping me more. But when I mentioned it to Max, he said:

"The payoff for me helping you is that you're more available to me. Why the hell do you think I do this stuff? I still don't like to, but if you're less upset and warmer, it's worth it."

Men *do* talk about being lonely. They *do* see their partners as often unavailable. They *do* feel last on a list of priorities, and truly don't understand why she lets so many other things get in the way. Men want to feel cared for. Along with love and passion, what men then want, most of all, is companionship — and many men say that is missing.

Will He or Won't He?

All projections make it clear that most women will continue to work outside the home. Most couples cannot afford to pay other people to do all of the cooking, cleaning, washing, ironing, and assorted other household tasks. Does she do it all? If not, how likely is it that he will participate? The following list may help to define what factors will affect men's response to "cleaning up the hut."

Her availability. Men want and need to feel special. Since most men do not have multiple sources for emotional support, if women do not act in ways that make men feel wanted, men will tend to feel left out, deserted, and isolated. Men do not need to be taken care *of*, but need to feel cared *for*.

When men feel this way, they are more likely to give in return. While men may not like to do housework (any more than women do!), they will do more and with less griping if they feel there is payoff for them. One thing that will increase men's level of participation in household management is a more available partner.

The age of the man and the history of the marriage. Men in their teens, twenties, and early thirties have grown up anticipating being in a relationship in which she will be working outside the home and he will be grocery shopping, cooking meals, and washing clothes. These men are more likely to see this as a normal state of affairs.

In contrast, men in their forties and fifties who grew up in traditional homes, and who perhaps have had traditional marriages, will tend to have more difficulty in adapting to wives' being away and expectations for their participation. Younger couples tend to have a more egalitarian relationship, at least until the birth of children, when very often renegotiation becomes the norm. (See chapter 7.)

Whether or not he views her maintaining of the house as a measure of her care for him. "Nothing says lovin' like something from the oven" is one of the many commercials that tend to link women's household tasks with caring behavior. If a man (consciously or unconsciously) links these two, then the fact that she is doing less can make him feel less cared for. This may be one of the times when an open discussion can be very beneficial. Most men can respond appropriately when they understand that the issue may not be one of her caring for him less, but simply a matter of too much to do and not enough time. Unless he is rigidly traditional, he will usually accept this explanation and be a more willing participant.

How strongly he encourages her career. Many men are enthusiastic about their wives working and not being full-time housekeepers. In those instances where men both understand and strongly support their partners, they are less likely to feel resentful of doing their fair share, and even more willing to pitch in without being asked.

How much housework he does. The most problematic of all systems is the one that depends upon a man to take *primary* responsibility for housework. The research evidence reported by Philip Blumstein and Pepper Schwarts in *American Couples* (see Suggested Readings) points out that many men become highly resentful when they're expected to do "too much." While there are certainly a handful of house husbands, they represent only a tiny minority and should not be seen as typical. Most men are willing to be a part of the system, but don't feel comfortable owning it.

They would much rather hire help than do it, and this appears independent of whether they hold liberal or traditional views. Somehow, men's role definition does not allow most of them comfortably to be the primary housekeeper.

Whether or not his mother worked, went to school, or had a significant role outside the home.

Men who grew up with working mothers are more likely to see having a working partner as a normal rather than abnormal state of affairs. He probably had to become more self-sufficient earlier. He probably saw at least some role sharing and so finds it easier to accept. Of course, the primary factor was what he observed his father doing.

What Dad did. Role models are important. If Dad ran the house as a fiefdom, expecting to be picked up after, the son is more likely to see this as appropriate male behavior. If Dad went shopping, did the dishes after dinner good-naturedly (with the children's help), and could run a vacuum cleaner on Saturday morning with the best of them, then this is likely to be seen as very normal behavior for men.

How much he did as a child. Did he make his own bed? Set and clear the table? Do the dishes? Mop the kitchen floor? Men who did these things as boys are much more likely to have an attitude that makes doing them as adults no big deal. Less likely to be happy helpers are men who had few responsibilities and were always taken care of by Mom and Sis.

While men move reluctantly toward shopping, cooking, and other culinary tasks and with great shudders into the bathroom with a johnny mop, in other areas they are changing with greater enthusiasm. Perhaps the most notable is the role of father.

VII

In the Nursery

On any given weekday morning, many of the cars stopping off at school or child-care centers are driven by men. Fathers as well as mothers now attend teacher conferences and spend part of their evenings checking homework. Fathers bring their toddlers to community swimming pools, putting on bathing suits and helping instructors teach their children to become water-safe.

Men feed babies, change diapers, and bring sick children to pediatricians' offices. It's not uncommon to see a man pushing a baby carriage, jogging with an infant on his back, or shopping with a child in the grocery cart. Some men even leave work in the middle of the day to attend a child's school performance.

Why is this happening? Two major social changes have moved men into parenting roles: the growing numbers of women moving into the workforce and the increase in divorce.

In most intact families, women work outside the home.

If she isn't available to be with the children in the evenings, during the weekends, or when they are sick, often he takes over. When marriages end, joint custody is often the outcome, and in many cases fathers are more involved with their children after divorce than before. Divorce is also creating a small but growing number of single-parent households headed by men.

There is another perhaps more compelling reason. The breadwinning-only role is slowly losing its appeal. Men are wanting to spend more time with their children. Sure, some men are merely joining the parenting bandwagon because it is the "in" thing to do. But many more want to be involved fathers because they remember how much they wanted to know their own fathers but never did.

As they move into expanded fathering roles, men are finding this new territory has problems of its own. Like women first entering the workplace, men often feel like foreigners in the parenting arena. Many say they don't understand the values, rules, and expectations of this world, which used to be pretty much "for women only."

The full subject of fathering is too extensive for me to cover adequately in a single chapter. Many excellent books, such as Martin Greenberg's *Birth of a Father* and Bob Greene's *Good Morning, Merry Sunshine,* have been written on this topic and are listed in Suggested Readings. What I want to explore here are men's feelings about fathering and what occurs between men and women as the men become more active parents.

The Relationship Problems When Dad Gets More Involved

Many men are much less comfortable with the *reality* of dealing with infant children than with the *fantasy*

105

of what it's going to be like. With good intentions they talk about what they're going to do after the birth of their child, but then find themselves in the awkward predicament of either not knowing how to carry though or not wanting to. Often they are reluctant to discuss these new feelings with their partners. Again, they say one thing but do another.

How do women feel when faced with this contradiction?

Men and women seem to have very different parenting styles. Particularly with infants, women tend to cuddle, rock, and coo, while men want to play. Mothers spend extended periods of time with their children while men are comfortable with shorter, more specific interactions. Even though both may be novices, mothers often end up instructing fathers on how to parent, her way. Most men resent this, and women continue to feel uncomfortable about the way that their partners parent.

What generally happens?

While men are participating more, most are not yet ready to be "equal" parents. Moreover, even if they wanted to, the mores of the work world and the demands for male career success make this unlikely.

Are there any hopes for change?

Although many men have become involved parents, there are still others who want a traditional family in which their children are raised by their wives. Many women married to these men hope that their attitudes will change.

Do they?

Let us first see what happens when a man's expectations of what he will do as a parent exceed the realities of what occurs. Take the case of Susie and Harry.

Why Can't I Count on You?

Susie, a thirty-five-year-old realtor-to-be, sat in my office and described what had taken place the previous weekend. Harry, her husband, sat beside her as she recounted the story.

"He knows how hard I'm working to pass the exam. He agreed to watch Andrea on Sunday right after breakfast. I told him that I really needed the time and that I was going to be meeting with a study group. Everything was settled.

"Then, as we finished coffee, he asked me when I'd be back. I told him one o'clock. That's what we had agreed on. He looked pained, so I said, 'Well, maybe I could get back a little earlier.' But inside I was really boiling. I mean, after all, this was the first time I had taken any time for myself, and here he was complaining already."

Susie's voice got louder. "Then as I was getting my books, he came up to the bedroom and said, 'What should I do with her?' I was furious. I told him *again,* 'Feed her, then put her down for a nap, and when she wakes up, take her for a walk.'

"He said, 'Feed her? What should I feed her?' "

She turned to Harry: "Dammit, Harry, we had had this conversation already and I'd even written down what to feed her. Then you began doing a number. I was angry then, and I still am."

Harry and Susie were not a couple that slipped unthinkingly into having a child. As I gathered information about their decision, I found that they had talked for over a year about whether or not to have children.

Susie was very clear with Harry that if they were going to have a child she was going to need his help. She and Harry agreed that she would continue working in real estate, both because they needed her paycheck and because she wanted to. Harry was agreeable and talked about how much he looked forward to having children. Before the baby was born, Harry told Susie how good a parent he thought he would be and how much love and affection he expected to give this unborn child of theirs.

Harry did all the right things during Susie's pregnancy. He went with her to Lamaze classes and helped check out child-care centers. He chose the crib. He went to the doctor's office for prenatal visits and attended the parenting seminar a month before Susie was due to give birth.

So what went wrong?

Harry said, "Well, I'm not really sure what the problem is, but I guess I have some idea. Susie is right in terms of what the *facts* are, but I don't think she told the whole story."

He turned to Susie: "Why didn't you say that I'd been asking you for the last week to talk with me about how to take care of her? Why didn't you tell him that every time I picked up the baby you told me that I was doing it wrong? You told me once I was going to drop her."

Harry seemed to pick up steam, and his words came out much faster. "Okay, maybe I don't hold her right, but I haven't had much practice.

"Yes, I was ambivalent about Sunday morning. First of all, the study session was supposed to be held Friday night. Then at the last minute you changed your mind, or something happened."

Susie began to talk, but Harry put up a hand and said, "As she got ready to go, she got more and more nervous."

Now he faced Susie: "Yes, you did. You began getting that uptight look, doing those uptight things, stacking your books, beginning to line things up, beginning to put the dishes away, all of that fussbudget stuff that

108

tells me you're really tense. Well, that got me really uptight too."

Harry was now speaking to me again: "So I figured I'd better make sure that I had things straight. I asked Susie what time she was going to be back because I didn't want there to be any confusion. She jumped right down my throat.

"The other thing was when I asked what to do, I really meant it. We had planned out Friday evening. I had not been with Andrea during the day. I just didn't know what to do."

Susie spoke at this point: "What do you mean, you don't know what to do? She's already *two months old*. She's your child too. You hardly spend any time with her. You pick her up for five minutes. She begins crying and you give her back to me or to the baby-sitter."

Harry had said all the "right" things. He even thought all the "right" things. He remembered his own childhood — how loving his mother was, how close he felt to his father. Harry was distressed that he hadn't had strong positive feelings toward his own child immediately. Susie certainly seemed to have all of those good feelings.

But he didn't. If he felt anything, it was *fear*.

Harry said, "I think the most surprising thing to me was that I was absolutely petrified the first time Susie gave Andrea to me. I *did* think I might drop her.

"Then I guess I held her too tightly and she began crying, and that panicked me even more, so I gave her back to Susie.

"Susie seemed pretty relieved to get her back, and Andrea seemed happy to be away from me. I guess that's how it began. I was uncomfortable then and I guess I still am."

Like so many other young couples today, Susie and Harry really felt a little overwhelmed by their situation. Susie felt betrayed, let down, and deserted by Harry. After all, what Harry had told her about what he was going to do was quite different from what he actually did.

Harry had really meant it when he said he was looking forward to the birth of their child. He didn't lie about his wanting to participate in her care. What he didn't and couldn't know was how he would feel when the moment finally came — the awkwardness, the discomfort, the frustration. And it never occurred to him to tell Susie about these feelings. At first, he didn't even realize he had them. Once he did, he felt too embarrassed.

But as Susie heard Harry talk about his apprehension and as Harry heard Susie acknowledge his situation and talk about her own, each became less angry with one another. This seemed to open the door for better communication.

After their anger had lessened, I told Harry and Susie that what they were experiencing was pretty typical for new parents today. Rather than talking about the "problem," they and many other couples like them tended to do what comes most naturally — blame and criticize each other.

In their situation Harry needed Susie to understand his lack of confidence and skill in caring for Andrea. But rather than expressing this, he simply avoided caring for her. Susie, on the other hand, assumed equal competence on Harry's part. Seeing his pulling back as sure evidence of his unwillingness to parent Andrea (the opposite of what he had professed earlier), she too became angry and acted out her anxiety and frustration.

Over the next months Harry and Susie (and Andrea) got along considerably better. As they described it, the key to their greater harmony was understanding that each was experiencing Andrea's first year of life in very different ways. They also spent more time talking about what they were experiencing, often finding their differences a source of humorous interchange. From what they told me, Harry did develop strong feelings about his daughter. It just took a little longer for him than it did for Susie. He also learned to play and care for her without Susie's close supervision. As Harry's fear diminished and his competence increased, Susie's frustration subsided.

Many Men Are Not Too Comfortable with Infants

What can we learn from Harry and Susie? Well, for one, many men seem to be less comfortable than women in dealing with infants. Why this is so requires a bit of conjecture. Part of it may be that, women being women, they usually have had more experience with children than most men — baby-sitting, caring for younger siblings, and so on. Even today, most parents of infants are more comfortable with girl baby-sitters than with boys. As a result of this increased exposure, women often come to parenthood with greater skill and ease. Some would also say that mothers are more relaxed with infants because they have had a nine-month prenatal experience that men obviously don't have.

Women tend to have greater resources available to them when some problem or question develops with their new baby. They have friends and an overwhelming array of articles in any given woman's magazine on children and child rearing. If something about her baby had concerned Susie, she probably would not have had a second thought about calling a woman friend, another mother, for advice.

111

On the other hand, if Harry had had the same concern, particularly in Susie's absence, how comfortable do you think he would have been calling a male friend, another father, for some assistance? Men are more likely to ask their wives or mothers for help rather than another mother, or God forbid, another father. Men's periodicals do not deal with parenting issues. In fact, men's magazines don't usually deal with relationship issues of any kind. Except for an occasional article, men read about business, sports, high fidelity, and sex, not about babies or children.

All new parents like Harry and Susie experience pressure and exhaustion in unique and different ways. With a new baby, particularly the first one, the easiest place to unburden your frustration is the other partner. Finding fault is easy. Talking with each other, being very descriptive of feelings and thoughts, is more effective.

Finally, it must be said (without being condescending) that new fathers often need to be eased into having time with their infant children. Because they are often lacking in skill, they tend to cope with infants better when the time they have together is initially limited (less than two hours) and structured (the mother or child-care person having laid out specifically what the normal routine involves). As their experience increases, so does their confidence and their capacity for extended periods of solo responsibility.

I'm Doing It My Way

In some cases, men find themselves running into what seem to be brick walls of expectations from partners. These expectations often are a reflection of what women themselves do as parents. "Do as I do or you're doing it wrong" is the unspoken message men often receive. Needless to say, this is not a particularly agreeable situation for many men. To see how it gets played out, let me introduce you to Todd and Margaret.

Todd is a forty-two-year-old CPA. He's tall with wild-looking, bushy hair, a mustache, and tends to look rumpled, even when his suit is freshly pressed. Margaret is also tall, dark, and attractive. At forty-three she has been a veterinarian in private practice for more than ten years. After a talk I had given on the differences between men and women, Margaret called me for an appointment. With her husband she came to the office.

She began: "I'm concerned about what's happening to our children. We have part-time child care and that helps, but it's not a substitute for parents. Whenever I'm not working, I'm with them. But Todd . . . well, he seems so casual about the whole thing. I feel that he needs to spend more time with the children. After all, they need a father as well as a mother."

Todd jumped in without being asked. "Margaret continues to tell me I don't do enough, that I don't spend enough time with them, and that even when I spend time with them, what I do is never right. I don't really know what's bothering her, but I'm really getting tired of her constant complaining. Frankly, I just think Margaret feels guilty about how much she works and how much she's not with the kids herself."

I asked Margaret how much time she did spend with her children.

"Whenever I'm not working, I'm with them."

I persisted and asked her how much time that was.

"Well, most evenings, usually Saturdays, and part of the day on Sunday."

Todd nodded in agreement. Then I asked Todd the same question.

"Well, actually," he said, "I think I'm with them as much as Margaret is."

Margaret interjected softly, "But you're not really with them!"

Todd retorted, "Of course I am!"

I asked for further explanation. It seemed that Todd and Margaret had worked out a reasonably balanced formula. Monday and Wednesday nights Todd would be responsible for the children after dinner. Tuesday and Thursday nights Margaret had them. But this his-and-her-night-out-with-the-kids solution did not seem to meet Margaret's expectations.

Margaret said, "Sure, Todd takes them. But he's not really with them. He's just in the same room. Our four-year-old is watching television, our seven-year-old is doing homework, and Todd is reading the paper."

Todd responded, "You know, not only do you want to control what *you* do with the children, but you want to control how *I* deal with them too. Justin is doing just fine watching TV, and I'm there and ready to help Mark. I check his stuff over.

"What I find most annoying is that you keep coming in from the other room to check up on me. Why don't you go shopping? Why don't you go for a walk? Why don't you read? Why don't you just get out of there for a couple of hours?"

Men and Women Parent Differently

Men say they are quite content to engage in parallel activities with their children. They may read the newspaper, for instance, while being available for help on homework. They may watch television while the children play board games on the floor nearby. Men are comfortable cycling in and out of activities with their children.

Most women, however, tend to be more continually involved with children for longer periods of time. They are more apt to sit down and help children with homework or play the board games *with* the children, for example. Many times women expect or want (or demand) men to do the same things. Not to carry though is perceived as a lack of fatherly interest and involvement.

Men rebel against those kind of dictates, particularly when it seems as though the children are satisfied. Anger and resentment emerge, and the important question of what kinds of attention children need becomes a power issue between the partners.

In the story above, Margaret wanted Todd to parent as *she* would parent. Todd wanted to parent in his own way. In fact, he resented Margaret's intrusion. He was criticized for doing it "wrong." Margaret also felt guilty about not giving enough time to her children and didn't understand why Todd didn't feel the same.

As I looked over at Margaret, it was clear she had stopped listening to Todd. Todd, too, had stopped listening to Margaret. They were in a conversation they had had many times before, each blaming the other.

You Need to Change!

To help Margaret and Todd begin dealing with their situation, I first pointed out that they were both engaged in a common misbelief: "Everything would be fine if the other would change."

As a clinical psychologist, I would say this is the most predominant theme I hear from those seeking help regardless of the issue. Perhaps because she herself was feeling so guilty, Margaret wanted Todd to change by spending more time with the children and to do it in the way she would. Todd wanted Margaret to change by leaving him alone while he was taking care of the kids (and perhaps by working fewer hours).

Even though it came through somewhat angrily at the time, I think Todd was wanting Margaret to change in another way — by taking better care of herself. Remember his saying something about doing things for herself? "Go shopping . . . go for a walk . . . read."

Each was so busy trying to change the other that Margaret and Todd lost sight of the fundamental point: they both wanted to be good parents to their children, and each wanted to feel loved and appreciated by the other.

Feedback Is Not Always What It Seems

As I continued to work with this couple, I tried to show Margaret that her attempts to "help" Todd parent were both presumptuous (only *her* way was the right way) and pretty ineffective. So often when we "give feedback," what we do is tell others what to do.

I always give feedback in a constructive, nonevaluative, nonjudgmental way that leads to a careful reassessment of the situation and subsequent behavior change.

You, on the other hand, are accusatory, attacking, negative and hostile. Is it any wonder that I resent it when you give me feedback?

This sums up how most people feel about feedback. We'd all rather give it than receive it. The more important the issue, the more pointed the feedback. It's really crazy, but often when we want to "help" someone with their behavior, we end up criticizing them or telling them what to do instead, producing reactions the opposite of what we intended.

Let's take a look at how Margaret's language affected Todd.

116

MARGARET'S WORDS: Todd needs to spend more time with the children.
KIND OF MESSAGE: An order, a command, telling him what to do.
TODD'S REACTION: Resentment.

MARGARET'S WORDS: After all, they [the children] need a father as well as a mother.
KIND OF MESSAGE: Guilt trip.
TODD'S REACTION: Anger, not activity.

MARGARET'S WORDS: But you're not really with them!
KIND OF MESSAGE: Judgment, perhaps a bit of moralizing.
TODD'S REACTION: Defensiveness, again not action.

Other similarly ineffective methods of communicating are threatening, name calling, accusing, sarcasm, and hostile silence.

In talking with Todd and Margaret about these interactions, Todd acknowledged that he was so defensive that he discounted Margaret's comments without even hearing them. They began to see why all their conversations seemed to end in arguments.

Let's take a look now at Todd's behavior. Was he being unresponsive to his children? Was he spending enough time with them? Was it "good" time? These are not easy questions to answer.

Ask the Kids What They Think

Since Todd and Margaret's children were four and seven years old and able to express themselves, I suggested something pretty simple: ask the children what they think about Mommy's and Daddy's time with them. Is it enough? Are they satisfied? What would they want

117

to change or have stay the same? (Of course, it wouldn't be possible to ask nonverbal children these questions. So a father of infants might want to ask a pediatrician or look to some parenting books for guidelines.)

The children were consulted and said that everything was fine except the seven-year-old asked Daddy to play with him more. I heard from Todd and Margaret about a year later and they mentioned that "things were a lot better." Both were trying not to change the other's behavior, although they reported that was a lot easier said than done. Old habits die hard.

What can we learn from Todd and Margaret?

Men often want to parent in their own way, not as pinch hitters for their wives. And, doing it differently does not necessarily mean it is wrong or ineffective.

Neither men nor women respond positively to criticism.

Changing someone else's behavior is very difficult. Demanding that your partner change his or her ways of parenting is not an effective solution to a problem you perceive.

Equal Parenting

Let's start with the term. Also called shared parenting or co-parenting, equal parenting is such a new concept that it doesn't appear in most contemporary dictionaries. As used today, it describes the process by which parents (married or not) share equally *all* the responsibilities associated with the physical and emotional care of their child or children.

The topic of equal parenting has been receiving a lot of media attention lately. Increasingly, we're hearing about young couples who create flexible work schedules so that each can spend time caring for their children. We read about paternity leaves and watch

TV fathers take time off from their work to be with their kids. Men describe intimate details of their initial fatherhood experiences. From these glimpses one begins to wonder if men are going to work at all!

Because of this, I think that a lot of women believe that equal parenting is now the norm for the majority of younger couples in the United States. More and more women are expecting their partners to share parenting responsibilities on an equal basis. Unfortunately, there is little evidence to suggest that men are parenting equally anywhere. Even in countries such as Sweden, where the government has supported paternity leaves for many years, less than 10 percent of the men who have this option act on it.

There are strong forces working against men's coparenting, beginning with the workplace. Even if a man wanted to participate as an equal parent, the mores of the work world dictate that he shouldn't. He should, first of all, pursue his career single-mindedly, letting nothing or no one get in his way, including his children. He should work long hours, including week nights and weekends, ignore his physical and emotional needs, travel and move as he is asked, and keep "moving up," thereby proving to his superiors his worth and to himself his adequacy. The work world generally acknowledges a man's family only as the family supports him in his work role. Further, even today, a man is highly suspect and a poor candidate for upward mobility if family issues affect his work.

Interestingly, women employees are forgiven their family orientation much more easily than men. For example, recently on Phil Donahue's program, Jane Pauley, co-host of the *Today* show, admitted (albeit somewhat embarrassedly) that she had not gone after an important overseas assignment at a time when she didn't want to be away from her young twins. She said that she was hesitant to reveal this for fear that her admission might be evidence of some lack of commitment to her career. She made the statement, nevertheless, and those around her — Donahue, his audience, and other female television correspondents — seemed both sympathetic and understanding. What do you think the reaction would have been to a similar admission by Bryant Gumbel, her male co-host? How do you think the powers that be would have responded to hearing that one of their male correspondents wasn't going after key overseas assignments because he wanted to be home for his children? Sympathetic? Understanding? Supportive? Not on your life!

A second set of forces works against men's having more to do with their children, particularly young children. These involve internalized images of "appropriate" male behavior. While it is certainly all right for men to be active parents, comfortable behavior for most is traditional *fathering* — part-time playing with, doing things with, spending time with, teaching, and perhaps feeding a child. For a great many men, to do much more, to coo, bathe, diaper, or spend long periods of time alone with a baby or child, is traditional *mothering* activity. Men are reluctant to take on any behavior that smacks of being female.

What Do You Mean, I'm Going to Be the Primary Parent?

In some cases, men are very clear from the beginning about not wanting to share parenting with their spouses. Not wanting to accept that, many women just don't believe their partners even when it is said many times over. Jack and Natalie are a good case in point.

In their early thirties, Jack and Natalie were living together and planning to get married. Jack was a manager in a retail department store. Over the years his income had steadily risen, so he felt secure financially and was interested in getting married and starting a family. Natalie also was interested in having children. She, too, was in retail sales, but with a company that sold women's cosmetics door-to-door.

In their initial session, I noted how happy Natalie seemed about her work and how unhappy she seemed to be with Jack.

She began: "Whenever I bring up the idea of having a baby, Jack says it's okay, so long as I am willing to cut back on my work hours to take care of the baby. He also tells me that he's not willing to change anything or even rearrange his hours to be available during the day. Can you believe it!

"It just infuriates me that Jack is willing to have the children if *I* do all the parenting. Look, I want to work! I really like what I do and I bring in a lot of money."

Jack shook his head as Natalie talked. He turned to me and said, "I tell you, she has a short memory. From the first time we started talking about children, three years ago, I told Natalie that if we were to get married and have children, I wanted her to raise them.

"She agreed with me then. I haven't changed my mind. What I'm saying now is no different from what I've been saying for years. She's the one who's changed. I don't know where all this equal stuff is coming from! Now she's angry at me because I won't agree to it."

Natalie retorted, "You're damn right I'm angry. Grow up, Jack, the world has changed a lot. Can't you see what other fathers today are doing? Look at your friends."

Jack said, "Look, I'm quite willing to go to Lamaze classes, and to be with the baby, and I expect I'll do homework and go to soccer games. But I am *not* going to share the parenting with you. I will not cut back at work. I don't want my child at a day-care center or with a baby-sitter all day long. If we're going to have children, then you'll have to be the person who raises them."

Natalie looked at me with disgust on her face. "Can you believe that? Not only am I to raise this nameless kid but I can't even get some help to do it!"

Jack interrupted her: "Wait a minute, Natalie. Don't put words in my mouth. No, I don't want my children to be brought up by someone else. Yes, of course, we'd have baby-sitters at times. I don't even mind having someone help you with the house so you can work part-time. I just don't want my child to spend most of his or her day, every day, with a stranger. I want our baby to be with you. Frankly, that's a compliment."

Natalie said to me, "I can't believe that Jack is still holding on to the old-fashioned picture of mothers at home baking cookies. My mother was one of those mothers. She had a master's degree in English but spent all her life as a housewife and mother. She was really unhappy. No way am I going to do the same.

"I'm not sure I want to have children if Jack won't really be a part. What are we going to do?"

Jack and Natalie's dilemma is more common than you may think. With all the publicity surrounding the issue of fathering, Natalie was not "off the wall" in thinking that most men are sharing parenting. As I have said earlier, it is a common misperception based on the fact that some men are doing significantly more.

First, I tried to give this couple a better perspective on the realities of men's involvement in parenting today. I talked with them about the unique pressures men feel from the work world, and from themselves, to stay traditional. I also pointed out that only about one man in ten is actually sharing parenting.

After discussing these issues with the two of them, I asked to speak with Natalie alone. I reminded her that Jack's feelings about wanting her to be the person raising their children had remained consistent. She apparently was the one who had changed her mind and expected Jack to change along with her. Because she felt strongly about this issue, it was easy for Natalie to believe that Jack's point of view was wrong or even crazy. We tend to do that, you know. In fact, the more powerful the feelings we have about an issue, the more certain we are that we are "right."

I made a second point to Natalie. Jack had been honest about his opinion, unpopular as it might be. She knew where he stood. As I have said before, few men are as clear about such controversial issues. Knowing from the outset what one is dealing with seems preferable to unanticipated change.

I reiterated to Natalie what I believed to be a fundamental truth of her relationship with Jack: he was not going to change his attitude or his behavior about how he wanted his children raised. For her to put any more energy in that direction was nonproductive. I reassured her that there was nothing inherently "wrong" about her wanting Jack to change. The wanting was just unlikely to work.

I saw that Natalie had three choices:

- To accept the circumstances, marry Jack, have a baby — and significantly reduce her work life.
- To decide not to have a baby, but to continue the relationship with Jack.
- To end the relationship with Jack and look for a man whose views about child rearing were more similar to her own.

Natalie and I spent time talking about how one goes about making such an important decision as this, deal-

123

ing with the positives and negatives of each choice. She wasn't thrilled with the options, but felt they were probably accurate.

I next saw Jack alone. He came in already knowing most of what Natalie and I had discussed. We began to talk about what parenting was going to mean for him and for *his* child, not for Natalie. This point had been lost in what had become a battle of "giving in" or "not giving in" to Natalie's desire for him to be an equal parent. I noted that it was pretty difficult to deal with these issues because none of us can know for sure how we are going to feel about a child until the child actually arrives. I also talked about how it was okay for Jack to feel as he did about equal parenting, and for Natalie to feel as she did. Neither had the corner on the "truth." (Couples often get into trouble when each thinks there is one true reality — their own.) Finally, I told Jack that now, or even after the birth of their baby, it was okay for him to change his mind about child care and about how much parenting he wanted to do. I told him that many middle-aged men often regret not having spent more time with their children during the growing-up years. I gave him information about the positive effects on both father and child of more fatherly time spent with children.

I said all this not to lobby for Jack's moving toward Natalie's position, but to give him from me, a man and a professional psychologist, objective information that might be useful in realistically appraising the parenting question for himself. (Jack and Natalie were still negotiating when I last met with them.)

The Quality of Fathering

Men's feelings about fathering are undergoing dramatic shifts. This is happening as a result of changes that women are experiencing as well as changes being encouraged by men themselves. The male role in parenting is being recognized as more important than we ever thought. Many more men are finding they truly enjoy the fathering experience.

How *do* men feel about fathering? How willing are they to participate? What kind of fathers are they likely to be? The answers to these questions will be as varied as the men responding to them. How an individual man will "father" will no doubt be a function and a reflection of his own background and is likely to be determined by some of the following things:

His own cultural heritage and whether his mother worked. The faces of fathering are many and varied, ranging from the exterior sternness of the Chasidic Jew to the warmth and loving expression of the Italian papa. If a man was raised in a two-career home and the parenting was not hired out, he probably saw his father diapering, hugging, and even feeding an infant brother. Having had this kind of experience, such a man is more likely to be comfortable and natural in fulfilling the parenting role, early and later on.

Experiences with his own father or other significant men. Men who were raised in a home with an absent father may find parenting more difficult to undertake. Having felt deprived themselves, some may say they intend to do more. But having no role model, they may also feel awkward. They may "give up" unless wives and others reward and encourage them to persist.

Whether he has attended parenting seminars, participated in prenatal classes, was in the delivery room, and had some opportunity to develop an early bond with his child. Men who have attended parenting classes and know more about children are more likely to be comfortable fathers. Many men are initially reluctant to attend classes (some do better at one-day events), but once involved they find the information practical, interesting, and intellectually stimulating. In the most positive circumstances, men view their capacity to parent as a new opportunity to demonstrate competence, which is often an incentive to participate. The earlier men have contact with their infant children, the more frequent this contact is and the more likely they are to be enthusiastic fathers.

The degree to which nurturing behavior is viewed as masculine. If a man has been raised to interpret holding, cuddling, stroking, soothing, or being tender as nonmasculine and masculinity is a dominant element of his self-image, he is unlikely to be a very effective parent with small children. "Masculine" men are often comfortable teaching children skills and values, but are rarely comfortable with outward expressions of love and warmth.

The cultural and social norms of his work environment. In Sweden, both men and women are given parental leaves. Some U.S. companies are moving in that direction. If men are given permission and encouragement to devote their energies to parenting, they will be more likely to do so. As our organizations and institutions begin to acknowledge parenting as a dual-gender experience, many men will find that it's easier and more comfortable to spend time with their children.

His partner's attitude toward his parenting attempts. Unfortunately, some women find themselves either fiercely protective of their own parenting prerogatives or highly judgmental of their partners' attempts. Since many men do not feel naturally at ease being a parent, they can be "turned off" parenting by being criticized for their efforts.

His career path and the amount of time available. If the father is a medical resident, in his first "real job,"

126

or on a fast corporate track, it is unlikely that his employer will offer any accommodations to his parenting role. He will no doubt have to put in more than full time to his job to prove his worth. Men who are "making it" in the work world don't want to jeopardize their primary male responsibility as breadwinner. Many might prefer to be at home with the kids. But if they must choose between the kids and success at work, work will win out.

VIII

Her Success: How Men and Women Cope

It was the spring of 1980, some six months after *Making It Together as a Two-Career Couple,* the book my wife, Marjorie, and I had written, was published. Our media tour was over and we were receiving an increasing number of requests to speak. On this day I had received many phone messages from Marjorie, but we had been unable to connect. However, the nature of the messages was that something special had occurred — something important and something good.

Finally, we managed to coordinate our schedules and were meeting for lunch. We came in separate cars. I parked and was walking toward the entrance of the restaurant when I heard Marjorie calling me.

"Mort, Mort." I turned around and there she was running toward me, smiling, obviously very excited.

"Guess what?" Marjorie said.

"What?" I replied.

"A big New York company is having their convention in San Diego and they want me to speak and do a workshop."

"Great!" I said.

"And you know what the best thing is?" she said.

"No."

"They've offered me a thousand dollars."

Marjorie waited expectantly for my congratulatory reaction, my enthusiastic response, my joining her in her moment of excited triumph.

She waited and waited and waited. Finally I said, "O-o-o-oh," and continued walking toward the restaurant.

Marjorie was, as she told me later, startled, upset, apprehensive, but mostly concerned about my reaction. We had talked about this issue many many times. In fact, we had even written a small section in our book dealing with what happens when women became successful. We had agreed that since this was a time when women's issues were being discussed and since Marjorie had been the first author on our book, she might get more requests for speaking and at higher fees than I would.

So I should have been prepared.

I had said all the right things. I had acknowledged that it made perfect sense for Marjorie to get speaking offers.

Since we had spoken about it, I should have been able to handle anything that came up and handle it well. In fact, I had dismissed even the *possibility* that I would be upset. After all, I was a psychologist talking to others about this very topic.

But when the moment of Marjorie's announcement came, I *was* upset. It was an instant reaction, one that did not take place after contemplation, evaluation, or reflection. My "Oh" was all that I could muster at that point. Fortunately, we did have lunch and immediately began talking about what had happened.

One thousand dollars was far more than Marjorie had ever been offered for a talk, and it was more than *I* had ever been offered. Here it was, the first big speaking engagement, and it went to Marjorie. The things I *thought* I believed vanished the moment I heard about the speaking fee. I was defensive, uncomfortable, and embarrassed at my response.

Marjorie was more prepared for my reaction than I had been. She told me that when she had gotten the phone call and accepted the offer, her pleasure was mixed with vague apprehension. She told me that when she called her father to tell him the good news, he too was concerned. They had the following conversation.

"Dad, this is Marjorie. I've just been offered a thousand dollars to speak at a convention right here in San Diego."

Marjorie's father: "That's wonderful! [Pause] What will Mort think? No, I didn't mean to say that. That's wonderful! [Pause] But what will Mort think? How will he feel?"

What did I think? How did I feel? More important, what do men think about successful women? How do they feel when women they are involved with become successful? Why should success for their partners be a problem when success for other men isn't?

To begin with, most men and women were socialized at a time when success for women was infrequent and somewhat unusual. Success was a man's prerogative. If a woman attained success she did so by being connected with, or married to, a successful man. She shared in *his* success. Her role was to nurture and support and encourage his career so that he might achieve and she might become part of his reflected glory.

Twenty-five years ago, most women went to work after completing high school. They took secretarial, waitressing, nursing, or sales positions. If women went on to college, they became teachers or social workers. While they could earn salaries that were at parity with those of men holding the same jobs, none of these occupations offered a level of economic return that was very substantial. Most women stopped working when they had children or certainly began working part-time. Work was only an "until" (i.e., until marriage or children) or an "in case" (i.e., in case of no marriage or widowhood or perhaps divorce) activity. The chances of women's becoming "successful" were slim indeed.

Very few women went to medical school, business school, dental school, or law school. Few women completed doctoral programs and rarely became university faculty members. When they did, they were often shunted into part-time positions or became lecturers and were not allowed to teach in the same departments as their professor husbands. Women did not become engineers or get MBAs or move up the corporate ladder. Women generally topped out at the first supervisory or management position.

Are things different today? Absolutely. There have been striking increases in women's involvement in preparation for the power professions — medicine, law, politics, psychology, dentistry, engineering, business. We are flown by women pilots, examined by women urologists, have our loans approved by women managers, are sentenced by women judges, and elect women senators.

It is fair to say that compared with twenty-five years ago the number of women who are "successful" has increased dramatically. It is also apparent that, given the current state of our society and economy, there is not going to be any decrease in the number of women in the work force and the likelihood of their being successful. Simply on the basis of sheer numbers we are going to be dealing with far more successful women in 2006 than we did in 1966 or than we do today. How are both men and women going to cope with this?

Recently I've been talking to a number of single women to get some sense as to their perceptions of how men respond to women's success. Many women tell me that at the beginning of a relationship they will lie (or not tell the *full* truth) about how successful they are.

For example, Marilyn, an attractive twenty-eight-year-old assistant professor, said: "I couldn't quite figure out what was going on. Very often I'd meet a guy and we'd seem to be getting on very well. He seemed to like me. I certainly liked him. We'd be having a great evening. Then, at some point, he would ask me what I did and I'd tell him.

"You want to talk about a turn-off! Somehow I find men become uncomfortable when I tell them that I teach at a university. Instead, what I now do is either avoid the subject on the first date or, if it does come up, simply say that I'm a teacher. After we've established some contact, I can then elaborate about what "teacher" means and then it seems to be okay. But at the beginning, it really tends to make it hard for us to get started."

I asked Marilyn how she felt about not being truthful.

She hesitated for a moment and then said, "I guess I do feel somewhat uncomfortable but I'm not quite sure what the alternative is. I want to have a relationship. I want to marry and have children at some point. But one of the things I find is that the men I meet seem to find my achievements a barrier. They don't see me, only my Ph.D., and the fact that I'm in a university. Somehow that's a negative rather

132

than a positive. Then they seem to ignore other parts of me. It's a real dilemma and I don't know how to resolve it."

How unusual is Marilyn's story? Not unusual at all, my women informants tell me. Another variant of minimizing success is what a film director told me she and many other single women do.

"When I meet a guy for the first time and he asks me what I do, I tell the truth, but then I downplay it and tell him that while I'm doing well at work, I'm a failure someplace else. Like, my apartment is a mess or I don't have time to exercise or even that I don't have much time to date. Somehow, it makes him more comfortable. The last thing I'd ever do is say that I've got it all together. The sad thing is that I don't like to hear me putting myself down, but I do it anyway."

However, the concern that many women have about being too successful is not restricted to single women. Indeed, since success for women sometimes takes longer for them, particularly if they've married and have taken time off for children, the problems associated with women's success are also likely to emerge as a couple's development unfolds.

In my clinical practice, I have seen an increasing number of men and women dealing with the issues related to women's success. Let us examine some of the most common situations and find out how men and women can cope successfully.

If He's the Spouse

Catherine and Paul had attended one of my two-career-couple seminars and eventually came to see me professionally. They were both in their late twenties, had been living together for two years, and had been married for one. They were bright and articulate and clearly cared for each other deeply. This evening in my office, they were obviously quite uncomfortable.

Paul began: "It was one of the funniest evenings I ever had. Well, not exactly funny. Weird. Catherine had asked me to go to her company parties for the last year, but for one reason or another we were never able to get one on the calendar. Last night was the first time.

"Catherine told me it was a special event. She was the only middle manager to be invited, since her division had the largest increase in sales over the last quarter. She was particularly interested in making a good impression.

"We were one of the last couples to get to the party and as soon as we opened the door I began feeling uncomfortable. There were two groups of people on opposite sides of the room. Just as we came in the door Catherine's boss met us, said hello, and then announced to everyone that 'Catherine and her husband' had arrived. Catherine immediately went over to the group on the right-hand side of the room. There were over a dozen men and one other woman and she became involved in a conversation.

"I didn't know what to do. It was obvious that Catherine was talking with her colleagues and I didn't feel I belonged *there*.

"Looking over to the other side of the room, I saw only women. I didn't feel like I belonged there either. I stood there for a second and then said to myself, 'Maybe I'd better go powder my nose.'"

The problem identified by Paul is becoming common for men today.

Paul thought it would be interesting to meet Catherine's associates. He was proud of her accomplishments. He was also, however, used to being at parties in which either he and Catherine knew most of the people there equally well (they were there as a couple with other couples, in other words). Or, if they were going to a business event, they were with *his* colleagues.

Now, Paul found himself in a new situation. He was the *spouse*. His wife was with colleagues, and he was there as her partner, as Catherine's husband. Not only that, but Catherine had been invited because of her achievements. When I asked Paul how things ended, he said he felt "out of it" throughout the evening. He was also upset at Catherine for having "put him in an uncomfortable situation."

In discussing the issue with this couple, I suggested that each of them might have to make some accommodations. It was going to be important for Paul to acknowledge that he would be continuing to be in situations where he would be with Catherine's co-workers. She had a career path and Paul *said* he was supportive of her achievements. Therefore, he could not at the same time refuse to participate in the social obligations that were necessary. He certainly expected Catherine to attend *his* business functions and would have been startled had she indicated a reluctance to do so.

I also suggested to Paul that he needed to anticipate that he *was* going to feel uneasy and perhaps take some steps to increase his comfort level. This might include asking Catherine to tell him something about the people who were going to be at the party, both colleagues and spouses, so that he would not be going into the situation so unprepared.

I pointed out to Catherine that she could be helpful. If she wanted Paul to be comfortable at events in which she was going to be the primary person, she needed to do some bridging for him. I reminded her that while most girls and women have had many years in which they learned how to cope with being at a party in which all of the guys knew one another, most men had not had similar experiences. It was important that she help him connect with two or three people so that he was involved in conversation before she went on to socialize.

My Wife the Star

What happens when a woman suddenly and dramatically becomes significantly more successful than her partner? What is it like for him when she is bringing home the majority of the income? How does he feel when she is the one who is getting phone calls or being interviewed? What is it like when she is away for days or perhaps weeks at a time? What does it feel like to be introduced as her husband when for the past twenty years he has had a professional identity of his own and has been used to having her introduced as his wife or to have them both introduced according to their professional achievements?

Frank and Barbara had been together as a couple for twenty-five years. They began as friends and colleagues, started dating, fell in love, and have been married for the past twenty years. In the beginning he was her mentor, five years her senior, an established attorney and partner in the firm. He helped her to sweat through the rigors of being a new associate in a large law office. He helped her deal with the frustrations of doing all of the work and seemingly getting little of the credit. He helped her accept the long hours, showed her how to do legal research, reviewed her briefs, coached her on courtroom procedures, and even went over her opening and closing arguments.

It all seemed to be working out well because he became a partner and she rose rapidly. She was bright, articulate, assertive, and competent, and she soon developed the respect of the other members of the firm. Eventually, she became a partner too. So it had all worked out for the best. Or so it seemed.

Then Barbara had a case that gained national recognition. It was an issue that touched the lives of many people. She performed very well and prevailed. Soon she was getting requests to discuss the case, first with newspaper reporters, then on the radio, and finally on television. She wrote a popular piece for a magazine, and was called to Washington to testify on a bill related to the issue.

Since the firm was getting many cases because of her high visibility, there were fewer expectations for her to be doing more traditional "legal" work. Eventually she was given a six-month "sabbatical" to continue writing and speaking on the subject and to complete a book that she had been asked to write.

And what about Frank? What happened to him? Well, nothing very much. He continued to function as a senior partner of the law firm, continued to be liked and respected by his colleagues and their friends, but clearly was not as well known or famous or sought after as Barbara.

It should be pointed out that Frank was not only a respected practicing attorney but had also written a series of important articles and a well-received book. Clearly, however, he was now married to a rising star.

In this case Frank had not failed. Indeed, he was continuing to succeed. However, his degree of success remained constant while Barbara had "taken off." In one of the men's groups that I hold periodically, Frank shared his own reactions to what had taken place.

It's as though I was living in two worlds at the same time. I kept saying to myself, "Isn't it great?

She really deserves it." I was even able to say it to friends and the people at work.

At the same time there was this feeling in my stomach — kind of empty and at times almost a nausea — particularly when she was given the sabbatical.

I just couldn't tell anyone how I was feeling. I was too embarrassed and angry at myself. So I just withdrew. When she asked me what was wrong, I said I was worried about some problems at the firm.

Fortunately, Barbara was great. She just went about her business and didn't make any big deal about what was happening. Finally, one night after we had been out to dinner, I told her what I had been experiencing and that helped a lot. But it took me awhile to get out of the pit.

Was Frank's reaction unusual? Was he simply over-reacting? After two decades of achievement, wasn't it somewhat inappropriate for Frank to be responding this way?

First, Frank's reaction was very common and very predictable. This is how most men react if they are suddenly eclipsed by their partners. Most men are most comfortable if they are in the dominant, or at least equal, position with their partners. Part of their discomfort is that they wonder if she will see him as less because she has become more.

Frank said he was embarrassed about how he was feeling. He doesn't talk personally with other men. He felt he couldn't tell Barbara. So he simply shut down. He pulled back. When questioned, he denied that he was upset.

Frank was unusual in that he was more aware of

what was going on than many other men are, and ultimately he was able to share what he was feeling with Barbara. What might have happened if he had not been aware of his feelings or had continued to isolate himself? What if Barbara had not been as unaffected by what was happening to her? Do marriages really break up because she becomes too successful? Yes, they do — but why?

Since men have been encouraged to succeed and their success has not been viewed as a problem, it doesn't seem fair that just because women are now doing the same thing it should be labeled a problem. In fact, it is precisely because we have been prepared, both men and women, for *men* to be highly visible and highly successful, that somehow a woman's success is aberrant.

I have talked with many couples about this issue. Some common themes are evident and some general recommendations emerge.

If possible, it's best that partners try to anticipate the woman's success and begin talking about how each is going to respond *before* it takes place. While this doesn't guarantee the transition will be a smooth one, at least it gives a shared reference point before the craziness begins.

Both men and women must work particularly hard at being able to maintain closeness during this time. Time to be together must be planned, and it is vital that the "success schedule" not rob the couple of a chance to be alone with no distractions.

It is important that both men and women understand that the excitement of success is sometimes, if not often, short-lived. (Barbara, for example, eventually did go back to practicing law and while she was still much more visible publicly, eventually their careers became more balanced.)

Men need to become more capable of both identifying and acknowledging feelings of hurt or abandonment. The dilemma for most men is being caught between their feelings of distress and their discomfort or shame over what they are feeling.

Women must understand that in most instances their partners will initially feel uncomfortable with their success *in spite of* what they are saying. Behavior is the key. When men become silent, withdrawn, or depressed, probably they're feeling both upset and embarrassed.

Of all the situations that I have described, nothing is more likely to threaten a relationship, even a very solid one, than an unanticipated, unplanned, sudden, and dramatic success of a woman. If this occurs when his career has peaked, the situation is more acute and professional help may be needed.

Midlife Mistiming

A new problem that has emerged as a result of women's returning to work: career cycling conflict. Consider a typical forty-five-year-old woman who married in her early twenties. She probably worked for a few years or went to school but then, if she had children, stepped out of the work force or worked part-time. For twenty years she was a full-time housewife, raising children, perhaps working part-time or volunteering at school or in the community.

Now her third child is eighteen and off to college or to work. She is free. What does she do? Well, not so long ago what she did was prepare for a second domestic role, that of grandmother. Then she got depressed. She stayed at home, perhaps got bored, and spent time with other women in similar circumstances. If she was af-

140

fluent, she went to a country club, played tennis, perhaps had a drink or two or three or more.

But now everything is different because men and more women are coming to view the departure of their last child, not as a time for depression, but as a time of emancipation! In record numbers they are going back to school for advanced degrees, picking up careers that had been put aside for many years, or reentering the workplace, perhaps at an entry level but with expectations of and desire for advancement. They feel unbound from the drudgery of housework, cooking, cleaning, and even children, and either hope or expect that their partners will be enthusiastic about their educational or career aspirations.

So, what about men? Well, twenty-five years ago most men began their careers and spent the better part of their lives moving toward positions of achievement and power. If they were fortunate they advanced and are now managers, department heads, successful professionals, or skilled craftsmen. As their wives enter their mid-forties these men are perhaps entering their late forties or early fifties.

They have achieved, many of them as much as they're going to, and have stepped back from the edge of competitive, aggressive work involvement. They know that they are going to be working for another fifteen or twenty years. But they also have become more interested in leisure time, relaxation, travel, and enjoying the luxury of moderate success. Just as these men turn their attention back to their partners, their adult children (or grandchildren), the trips they've deferred for many years, they find that things have changed.

How do these men feel when their wives are now *initiating* careers or educational plans that are demanding, that take time, and take "priority"? How do

141

they feel if their partners become moderately or even very successful? How do they feel when *she* goes away on a business trip?

When middle-aged men talk about their wives going to work and becoming successful, they often *begin* by sounding quite reasonable. Take the case of Tom.

Tom is a fifty-eight-year-old self-made man. He worked his way through engineering school, started his own business when he was twenty-three, and built it up rapidly so that at age thirty-four he was bought out by a major company and was "prematurely" wealthy. He continued to do well but never quite as spectacularly as he did originally.

He and Samantha met when they were both undergraduates. She completed her bachelor's degree (with honors) while pregnant and at one point it was a question whether or not their first child would be born before or after Samantha's degree was granted. When Samantha was forty-five, and the youngest of her four children was seventeen, she took a year's worth of graduate zoology courses (getting all A's) and got admitted to medical school. She did a residency and was then asked to join the faculty. This led to *extensive* discussions between Tom and Samantha.

TOM: You know, when Samantha first broached the idea of going to med school, I was surprised but I figured, why not? I mean, she had been there for me during the time that I had been going to school and starting the business and she certainly put in her time with the kids. I thought that it made sense for her to have her shot and I was very supportive during the time that she was in school, even during the residency.

One of the things that we had decided was that she would specialize in dermatology because that would allow for her to have a more controlled practice without emergencies and night calls. Also, she could work from part- to full-time, depending on the circumstances.

I didn't think that she would become quite as involved as she did or that she would do as well as she did. I'm all for her being a physician and I'm all for her practicing. But now this university thing has come up. She'll not only be at the clinics during the day, but she'll be writing papers at night. They've asked her to coordinate a research program, which means she'll be traveling at least twice a month. I was anticipating that now the kids are gone and we've got some time, we could do some more traveling and have more time for one another.

I'm not pleased with Samantha's desire to do more and I don't want to spend the next fifteen years of my life snatching time between her patients, conferences, lectures, or travels.

Tom is in a very different place from Samantha's. He has gone through the wars and battles of career success. He is middle-aged, active, and vigorous. He does not want to spend his days and nights at home by himself waiting for Samantha's return.

Intellectually, he knows that she is excited about her career and he knows that it's a wonderful opportunity for her. But he feels resentful and deserted, and guilty for feeling that way. Tom would rather he felt otherwise, but he doesn't. Samantha, a gregarious, energetic, attractive, outgoing woman, was between anger and tears.

SAMANTHA: Everything that Tom says is true, but I can't help how *I* feel. When I first started medical school, I knew it was going to be hard. But I never thought it was going to be this *interesting*. I never imagined that I would ever be good enough to be on the faculty.

Tom is absolutely right. I chose dermatology because it's one of the few specialties which doesn't tend to have night calls or emergencies, and the thought was I could either be a backup member of a private practice group or work part-time in a clinic.

Now I'm really feeling caught. I love Tom and I don't want to have anything jeopardize our relationship. He was very supportive of me while I was in school and during my residency. But I love my work and I love the opportunity. I really don't know what to do.

Many women share Samantha's dilemma. While going back to medical school at forty-five is unusual, it is not unusual for women to go into other work at that age. Interestingly enough, if they're competent and devoted, by the time they reach their early fifties they often have been promoted and are on a real career path. However, in order to pursue their career, they are being asked to put in more time, to travel, and to do the things that successful men have always done.

Many middle-aged men are sharing Tom's experience. They have been hell-bent on career success ever since they got out of school. They've built businesses, become senior managers or partners in law firms, or have established professional practices, or perhaps have simply reached a level where their income comfortably takes care of their expenses. Their children are out of the house, in college or working, and they are psychologically ready to relax. They may have spent little time with their children or their wives during the past twenty years because of how much time and energy they've devoted to their careers.

If they were indifferent fathers, they may be looking forward to being participatory grandfathers (all of the fun, none of the responsibilities). The house or the apartment seems empty with no children around, and, if they can avoid the crisis of midlife, they seem ready to develop the relationship that they had with their wives, which started during courtship and perhaps had not been looked at for many years. The Toms are now eager for intimacy and recommitment.

In many cases, neither men nor women accurately anticipate what can occur when a woman gets involved in work or school. The career time warp occurs because most women's careers begin to take off at the same time that most men's careers begin to wind down. Men now want to have their wives and partners more available to them. What can be done?

In Tom and Samantha's case we worked out an initial "negotiated settlement." Samantha accepted a half-time appointment with the university and was responsible only for the research project. This allowed her to have periods of time when she would work long hours and other times when she could be free to travel with Tom. She didn't feel that she was compromising the quality of her work, and she still was able to have the time for Tom and their relationship.

Tom was agreeable. He was still feeling some distress about Samantha's limited availability (the eight-week cruise was out!), but he was also feeling guilty that he was not supporting Samantha's full-time option.

The kind of problems that Tom and Samantha faced are beginning to increase in frequency. Both Tom and Samantha were acutely aware that if Samantha's career continues to make more demands upon her time, this is going to put a significant strain on their rela-

tionship. They see their marriage at this point as frag-
ile *and they're right.*

The Toms need to decide whether they want to end
their marriages and try finding another partner who
is as interesting and compatible as Samantha or modify
their expectations about what their life was going to
be like at fifty. This may mean reinvesting in a career
or some other option.

For the Samanthas, the ultimate decision may be
whether to be maximally successful and possibly be
alone, or less career-oriented and still married.

When Women Travel

One thing has become clear. Success has both payoffs
and trade-offs. On the plus side, success generally means
more money, more visibility, more prestige, more power,
more control. By the same token, success carries with
it a set of expectations. If you're successful, you are
going to be working more hours and putting in time
on evenings and weekends. If you are successful, you
are going to be traveling, since in today's world travel
is a part of achievement. All these trappings of success
have significant impact on men.

Perry is a forty-two-year-old architect. He has been
married to Ann, an interior designer, for twelve years.
They had decided that while they shared common in-
terests, they were too competitive to work together.
Therefore, except for an occasional "fun project," most
of the time they worked independently.

Both Perry and Ann have done well. They have two
children and have maintained a rather good balance,
sharing housekeeping and parenting and enjoying a
full social life. But things were beginning to change.

146

PERRY: I'm almost embarrassed to be talking about this but what's true is true. When we first got out of school, it was clear that my career was primary. I was putting in sixty to seventy hours a week. Originally, our dining-room table was only used for blueprints. I worked my tail off. There was a payoff too, because, as you know, I became a senior architect and then eventually got my own business started.

Ann has done very well and the company she works for has done very well too. Now they've branched into designing law offices and she has become really well known. Ann is the best there is — not only is she the best interior designer, but she really works well doing presentations. So they've been asking her to help get new business.

What does that mean? I'll tell you what it means. First of all, it means she's putting in more and more time. But worse than that, she's now gone at least once a week, sometimes for two or three days. Life is chaotic. It's hard on all of us and I feel lonely.

The other thing, and I guess I'm really embarrassed about this, many of the times she travels with two associates from the office and they're both men. I've never been jealous, but it does make me feel uncomfortable that Ann is spending nearly as many nights with them as she's spending with me.

I know when you've got a good relationship affairs aren't supposed to happen. But still, she's an attractive woman and I do worry. I know she must have felt the same way when I was traveling. But that was ten years ago.

It may be irrational.

It may be inappropriate. But, at this point, I'm

feeling her success is bringing us more problems than benefits and I don't know what to do about it.

Perry had made the right first step by acknowledging what he was feeling, talking with me about it. Many men don't. Women become upset when they hear about concerns like Perry's because men appear to have a double standard. What was good for men no longer seems to be appropriate when it applies to their wives. Most men will acknowledge it's not rational, but that *is* how they feel.

It is also true that sexual fears are not entirely without foundation. Affairs between women and men in their forties and fifties are occurring with greater frequency, and work is one of the most usual places for these relationships to begin. Alice Sargent, author of *The Androgynous Manager,* encourages men and women who travel together to discuss this problem as a way to minimize the likelihood of its occurring.

In this instance, the solution that was worked out was easy. I encouraged Perry to talk with his wife about some of his fears and concerns regarding sexual fidelity. She responded with great warmth and said she was not at all interested in a relationship with anyone other than Perry. This was a great relief to Perry. Ann also reminded Perry that the travel schedule was only going to be for another few months. She was developing a model for presentations that other staff people could use. She was already committed to limiting her travel to no more than once a week.

Reassured and encouraged, Perry developed a much more positive approach to Ann's absence. He used her time away as an opportunity to spend more and better time with his children. The last time I saw them they were doing well.

Coping Considerations

While many things influence how a man will respond to a woman's success, I will attempt to characterize those factors which are likely to influence men's responses. Looking at these will allow both men and women to determine with greater accuracy whether or not her success will be a problem for him and them.

The quality of the relationship. As in other areas, if a couple's relationship is tenuous, strained, and unhappy, the woman's success is likely to be one further element of stress, adding yet another problem to be dealt with.

Logistical complications. As said before, one of the trappings of success is travel. In most instances, the woman's traveling has a greater impact on a couple than the man's, particularly if there are children. Even in situations where men take a very active role in parenting, if a woman is gone frequently or for extended periods of time, it puts a special kind of strain on family relationships.

His career — where it is and where it's going. The more successful a man is, the less likely he is to be uncomfortable with his partner's success, even when it matches or surpasses his. If he has all the trappings of power and prestige, he may be less uncomfortable when she has them also.

In addition, the slope of his career will often influence how he is responding to her. If he is still on the rise, her success is likely to be less distressing. If, however, he has plateaued or had his career suffer a dramatic and significant reversal, then her success will be less easy for him to accept. Moreover, if in his own estimation he has not achieved the success he hoped for by the time he hits his forties, his ability to deal with his partner's success could be seriously impaired.

149

His self-esteem. Is he somebody who generally feels good about himself? Is he a self-confident, independent person who interacts easily and comfortably with those around him? If so, he is much more likely to deal with her success in a positive fashion.

His competitiveness and need to control or dominate. Being competitive and trying to win is a trait that most men are encouraged to develop. Being dominant and in control are also behavioral styles that are rewarded in the workplace and in media portrayals of men. Men whose need to win is predominant, who cannot tolerate losing at anything, including a friendly game of tennis, will have more difficulty. Those men who always have to win may feel they also have to win at home and will somehow interpret her success as his failure.

His personal history regarding successful women. If a man has grown up with a successful mother who had a good relationship with his father, he is much more likely to view female success as normal. If his own early history was staged by a very dominating father and a very submissive, passive mother, then this will be the early stereotype he brings to his relationship.

Again, while neither men nor women are bound by their history, neither can it be ignored. For both men and women, knowing something about their own and their partners' parental and family history will be a great aid in beginning to sort through how he may be responding to her success.

How she is handling her success. Both women and men can behave in ways that are clearly irritating and insulting and can exacerbate a situation. If she becomes unpleasant, withdrawn, arrogant, and denigrating, certainly he will respond in kind.

Some women, because of their family history, do have difficulty when they become more successful than their partners, interpreting their success as his failure and

150

responding in ways which are ineffective. A woman may become so self-involved that she forgets the needs of her partner.

The suddenness of her success. We are amazingly adaptive organisms. Given sufficient time, both men and women can accept many changes in their relationship. Imagine what would happen if in a period of one year we changed from looking like a twenty-year-old to looking like a sixty-year-old. That would be devastating. However, we gradually adapt to graying hair, a less firm jawline, and a less rapid recovery from a late night out. The same is true for success. If there is a slow and gradual buildup of her greater success, he is more likely to adjust in an appropriate fashion. If, however, she suddenly and dramatically leaps from one level to another (law student to law partner, extra to star, management trainee to assistant vice president for sales), then the coping and adjusting become more difficult.

How often and how well they can communicate about this issue. Talk helps. *Talking* — not comparing, boasting, or announcing — and talking about things that are difficult help even more. Being able to talk about her success in a way that makes it simply another issue to deal with is likely to depolarize them both.

Finally, the degree to which she behaves in ways which let him know that he's a priority. Both men and women can become overly involved in their work and career and give lip service to their relationship. However, one of the times when it's most critical for a woman to behave in ways that make a man feel that he has priority is the time when she is significantly more successful than he is. Many successful women with solid relationships acknowledge that they put even more effort into this aspect of their lives than they did before they achieved their success.

IX

New Beginnings

$\mathbf{M}$y goal in writing this book has been to lower the flood-waters of mistrust and confusion that currently exist between the sexes.

I've tried to portray men as they are today... strengths, weaknesses, virtues, faults, and all. Hopefully, I have dispelled a few long-standing myths:

- that men don't really need women
- that men don't want to commit
- that men don't want to marry.

But hopefully, too, I've also helped to dismantle the other set of misperceptions that were spawned in the ideals of the sex-role revolution:

- that men have become skilled at sharing feelings
- that men are willing to take on major responsibilities on the home front
- that men are prepared for egalitarian relationships.

They are moving in these directions but much more slowly than women may think or want.

- Men are still lagging behind in the nurturing, intimacy, emotional expressiveness areas.
- Men of all ages still respond first to how a woman looks, and second to who she is.
- Men, at the beginning, are still more likely to be charmed by a tender touch, rather than a brilliant thought. They do search for more as things continue.
- Most men are still uncomfortable being in relationships where women dominate (as are most women), but are gradually giving up the need always to be in charge.

Relationships

As I said at the outset, there has never been a more difficult time to have a relationship. Remember, though, we are standing on the shaky ground of rapid social change. So if you've been thinking that relationships are hard, well, you're right. But, if you've been thinking that yours is uniquely hard, you're probably wrong.

If you've been thinking (whether you're a man or woman) that it might be better to go back to the good old days when things seemed easier, don't be shocked. You're not alone. But if you know what it was *really* like, "way back when," you might not be so nostalgic. While roles may have been more clearly defined, most men were work-obsessed, most women one-dimensional housewives. Things were difficult then, too, but may have been less interesting.

If you think that it is virtually impossible to find anyone that is truly happy these days, and point to the fact that 50 percent of all marriages now end in divorce to prove your point, think again.

The divorce rate has stabilized, and living-together arrangements are now alternatives for the early marriages of twenty-five years ago, masking the real numbers of men and women who are coupled. Given the complication in today's world, perhaps what is remarkable is that half of all married couples *do* stay together.

Attitude

I began by emphasizing the importance of understanding as a starting point for working things out. To conclude, I would like to leave you with several tools, some *attitude guidelines,* that may assist you to use that understanding, help you to sustain your relationship, and head off abrupt terminations.

First, *recognize that conflict is a normal part of relationships and of life.* It comes right along with passion and deepening intimacy. Disagreement doesn't mean that a relationship is flawed. Never resolving anything, however, means that you need to learn more effective ways of navigating. Some of the examples given in previous pages may give you direction in developing techniques to deal with conflict.

Second, *stop trying to win.* Most men and women when faced with differing views about an issue, gear up for battle. Instinctively they first try to defeat the other, to stand triumphant. Usually, both lose. Skilled partners pass through this phase of confrontation quickly and then concentrate on solving the problem rather than winning the war.

Third, *accept that men and women are different.* They may also need different things to feel enriched. Sex therapists say, for example, that men like firm caresses, women more gentle ones. When men touch women vigorously or women touch men tentatively, neither is satisfied. The skill is to ask what is wanted, to state what you need, and to fulfill those requests with enthusiasm, expecting no less from him or her. This obviously goes beyond sex into all aspects of relationships.

Finally, *strengthen your tolerance for tension.* In this age of instant gratification, there is a tendency quickly to abandon things that aren't working perfectly, rather than trying to discover and correct the problem. Many today are good sprinters, but need to develop the capacity to run the long race. While I certainly don't advocate that men and women stay locked in continual conflict to demonstrate commitment, there needs to be some tolerance for tension, else one will continually be searching for the mythical sea of constant tranquillity.

Getting Help

Sometimes, even when you are doing your best, for one reason or another you may have exhausted your resources to move ahead. Before resigning yourself to a joyless status quo, a painful separation, or some other similarly undesirable outcome, you may wish to seek the assistance of a professional psychotherapist skilled in relationships. Years back, such a step would have been tantamount to admitting failure. Today, fortunately, looking for a relationship guide is viewed with much greater acceptance. Remember, most men and women come to relationships with little knowledge, other than what we saw our parents do — and they may not have had the skills or knowledge to be good role models. Few of us have had any instruction on how to relate to another person, so learning from an expert can often help.

What's Ahead

As I look toward the future of relationships I am hopeful. I see women learning to balance better the pulls of work and home. I see men becoming more able both to give and to get affection — from and to their lovers, friends, and children.

Men are beginning to give up their one-dimensional lives of work and achievement. While they continue to measure their self-esteem on the basis of career success, family has finally emerged as a second major force in their lives. Women have stepped back from the stridency of early feminism and are becoming more comfortable with both achieving and loving. The push for total self-sufficiency has faded, and they are now looking for balance.

Both men and women are moving away from the narcissism and self-centeredness of the previous two decades and are rediscovering the richness that comes with closeness and dependency, even though it carries with it the uneasiness of vulnerability.

Tomorrow

Many things, however, may be permanently changed.

Men and women will increasingly choose living together as an alternative to marriage. Divorce will become a permanent part of the landscape — but without the stigma, or at least with less of the stigma of the "failed" relationship. It will be more usual to have three or four mates in a lifetime rather than one. A lifelong, monogamous relationship will be only one among a number of equally accepted and viable alternatives. (The one worry in all this is the impact on children. Perhaps "parent" will become a functional rather than a biological term.)

However, men and women will continue to search for one another. The bursts of passion, the dance of courtship, and the fulfillment of a deep, loving relationship will remain with us. The Garden of Eden may look different in the future, but it will continue to flourish.

X

The Last Word
Marjorie Hansen Shaevitz*

Chances are that you have just finished reading the last chapter of this book. In reflecting back on what *Sexual Static* has been all about, I think that you will find you have learned a great deal about how men have been reacting to the changes going on in women's lives.

The most important theme in this book is that many men are feeling lonely — pushed out, abandoned — as their women have adapted to cultural changes by adding on new roles, increasing their activities, and unwittingly becoming less available to them. Mort, very appropriately, has declared this the overload-loneliness dilemma.

* Marjorie Hansen Shaevitz is not only Morton Shaevitz's wife but his business partner too. Together they co-direct the Institute for Family and Work Relationships in La Jolla, California. In addition to writing and speaking. Ms. Hansen Shaevitz also sits on California's State Commission on the Status of Women and was one of thirteen women chosen to represent the United States on the first all-women's trade mission to Europe.

158

As mental health professionals, Mort and I are convinced that with enough information any behavior or set of behaviors makes sense. The whole of this book has been devoted to describing contemporary American men and making some sense out of how they feel and why they act as they do today. Although in a previous book (*The Superwoman Syndrome*) I have described contemporary American women and attempted to make some sense out of their "superwoman" behaviors, in this epilogue I will try to provide some new insights into why women continue "to do it all," how they unknowingly are contributing to men's loneliness, and what part they play in perpetuating the Perfect Misunderstandings that occur between the sexes.

Much of what I write about will describe women in relationships that are beyond the dating or courtship phase or who are not currently in a relationship. This is not meant to ignore those of you who are in one of those stages. Keep in mind that what you read about now may help prevent difficulties in a relationship at some later time.

One of the most confusing aspects of what is going on with men and women is that a great deal is changing at the same time that much is staying the same. And speaking of change: for some people, particularly women, it's coming too *slowly*. For others, namely men, change is coming too *quickly*.

Even though sometimes it's difficult to discern who wants what, it is women, by and large, who have been unhappy with the inequitable distribution of roles and work in our culture. Women have wanted to change the rules not just of the home, but of the business world too. And women have wanted men to want the same things.

Many of us have assumed that they did. After all,

we have thought, it is only "right," only "fair," only (if you will) "downright American" to begin sharing the work in and outside the home.

But confusion has reigned because men have been giving us conflicting messages. On the outside, they have professed support for our liberation and the changes that accompany it. But on the inside, because of how they have been raised as males in this culture, they don't understand what is wrong, or why we should be so upset, let alone what they as men should do about it.

It's also difficult for us women to understand that, because of how we have been raised as females in this society, we feel responsible for and do automatically so many things in the relationship, household, parenting, areas that men never even think of. It's so easy for us women to judge that because they are not doing these things (even when we ask them to, once, twice, or a few times), our men are stubborn, uncaring, insensitive, or chauvinistic. We rankle with disbelief every time we hear them say they "don't remember," or "don't notice," or worse yet, "don't care."

I can't tell you how long it has taken me to understand that what dominates my thoughts on a daily (and nightly) basis rarely or never occurs to my husband (and most other men). Men and women have thinking and feeling worlds that are as different as night and day.

He doesn't:

- notice messy rooms, dustballs, or moldy food in the refrigerator
- hear the children cough or cry at 3:00 in the morning (when I am in the house)
- worry about what we'll do for dinner tonight, and

160

- whether there is food in the house to make it (he might think about what he'd like to do on his way home from the office, but never start worrying about it at 2:30 in the afternoon)
- anticipate who and what will be on our Christmas/ Channukah shopping lists in October, or even in December
- offer to a dinner hostess to bring something for the meal or remember to bring her a gift or to send a follow-up thank-you note
- concern himself about whether the linen or kitchen or clothes closet or any drawer is organized
- feel guilty if he doesn't keep in touch with close friends or family every few days

or

- think of any of the above in the midst of making love.

And, of course, *I* cannot let go of whatever he doesn't notice, hear, worry about, anticipate, offer, remember, concern himself with, feel guilty about, or think of.

When I have talked with busy women friends or patients about these things, I often discover that we have experienced a similar internal dialogue with ourselves that goes something like this:

I am overloaded . . . my work, the house, the kids, the shopping, the meals, the laundry, my friends, my parents. Why doesn't he help! How can he just let me do it *all!* Doesn't he see how exhausted I am all the time?

Most of us are incredulous that *he* is apparently so unsympathetic to the crisis we feel our everyday lives are in, let alone not do anything about it. You and I can be easily unaware that men's upbringing teaches

161

them to be oblivious to those aspects of living that so overwhelm us. The internal dialogue continues:

I would *never, ever* leave him abandoned to deal with all of this. *I* care about *him. I* would help *him,* pitch in with whatever he needed.

Because we have been brought up to notice what is happening to those around us, especially those whom we care for and love, it is natural for us to assume that the men in our lives also have this same capacity. Often we apply to him our own internal standards of appropriate feelings and behavior. How easy it is for us to expect from him what we would do if the tables were turned.

Let me also point out that our internal dialogue is usually just that, silent and private. Many of us don't tell the men in our lives what we're thinking. We don't want to impose. Above all, we don't want to antagonize. What we hope is that he will understand us, notice what we need, and spontaneously act on it, without our ever having to feel our guilt or his wrath in asking him. After all, other women do that, *he* did it while we were courting, and we are sure that Phil Donahue does it for Marlo. And the internal dialogue goes on:

Well, if he is just going to sit there and do nothing (or lie there, or go off on his own), then he must not give one whit of care for me! How can he tell me one minute that he loves me and then not do anything to help me!

These last words bring up an interesting psychological dynamic that has developed in women over the years. It has to do with the blurring of, and equating, the terms of *CAREGIVING* and *CARETAKING.* In everyday, real terms, here are some examples of these very different kinds of behaviors:

CAREGIVING BEHAVIOR	CARETAKING BEHAVIOR
Listening to a partner talk about his difficult day.	Discussing errands that need to be done.
Baking his favorite lemon meringue pie.	Preparing the evening meal.
Sending him flowers.	Planting the spring flowers.
Leaving a note in his car that says "I love you."	Leaving a note in his car reminding him to pick up the cleaning.
Planning a surprise, getaway weekend for him.	Arranging for the family vacation.
Buying him a special gift.	Shopping for household items.
Having his car hand washed and waxed.	Cleaning up the house.
Inviting *his* friends over for dinner.	Inviting *your* friends over for dinner.
Spending time alone with him.	Cleaning up the garage together.

Because women have been raised to be other-, not self-oriented, this blurring of caregiving and caretaking has probably taken place unconsciously as a way of our justifying how and why we spend our time. You see, in our culture we have been trained to put the needs of others first or feel guilty. So as we engage in our everyday caretaking activities (which take up a lot of our time), we cannot, psychologically speaking, tolerate "doing it for me." So if not for us, for whom do we do it? Of course, we caretake for him (or for them, if there is a family involved).

163

By the way, this might give you some idea about why many women are so resistant to (or feel guilty about) paying or asking someone else to do house caretaking activities. It feels to them as though they are giving up some of their caregiving.

This explanation also gives us a clue as to why so many men say they are lonely these days. We all know that more women are moving into the work force. Yet whether they are married or living with a partner, most women still continue to provide 85 percent of all caretaking functions. They "work" at work and then "work" at home because, after all, clothes need to be laundered, shopping taken care of, errands run, birthdays remembered, meals prepared, and dishes washed. Even if you lower your standards, certain things have to be done once in a while.

We, not *he,* feel responsible for taking care of all of these things, and so we busy ourselves with activities often from early in the morning until late into the night. In our minds, as we are doing this caretaking we are "taking care" of him.

Actually, some women are uncomfortable with the potential intimacy promised in caregiving. So they substitute, almost totally, caretaking activities for caregiving. One patient of mine kept herself busy *all the time* to avoid getting close to her husband and even her children. Another patient resisted all my attempts to help her deal with "overload" because we found that her merry-go-round of activities allowed her to avoid dealing with the problems of a relationship that had soured years before. Engaging in caretaking activities is such a convenient way of running away from ourselves, or from a difficult person, or from an unsatisfying relationship.

Meanwhile back in the den or the family room or the study or the bedroom, *he* sits there alone with the

TV or the newspaper or a book or a computer and wonders "what in the hell is she doing." *He* does not equate house caretaking with caregiving to him.

He calls to us, "Come sit with me and watch TV." *He* says, "Come talk with me." *He* asks, "Come make love with me." *He* doesn't understand why it appears that we would rather be doing all of this caretaking stuff than be with him. *He* yearns for the emotional caregiving that only we can provide him. And the busier we get, the lonelier *he* becomes.

I must say that it has just been recently that I have understood how enormously dependent men are on us for emotional sustenance. They want and need all the love and affection and comfort and support and nurturance they can get from us as individuals because we are "it" — their one source.

There is another dimension to caregiving in our culture that is particularly difficult for women. Men have not been raised to feel responsible for giving care to us, except under the specific circumstances of courtship and as a part of lovemaking. Without really being conscious of it, men don't feel responsible for reciprocating the support and nurturance that we so easily give them. But we want them to.

One of the new developments of this working-woman age is that we have less time (or take less time) for other women in our lives. Many of us have moved away from women friends, our traditional sources of support and nurturance, and have come to look for exclusive caregiving from the men in our lives. How often I have heard myself say, "I don't have time for my friends now. I'll get back to them after the kids grow up." Not until now have I realized that I was denying myself that special understanding and support that only other women can provide me. In many ways, women are now looking to men for what they have not been trained to

165

give us. Like the Adams of this day, many Eves have become *lonely* too.

So here we are, men and women alike, in the so-called enlightened age of the eighties, all working too hard, feeling lonely, and having no other explanation except to find fault with the person to whom we are closest, our partners.

At this juncture, let me be very clear about one thing. In describing the current-day dilemmas we women and men face, I, like Mort, am not pointing the finger of blame at either sex. Neither am I endorsing the status quo nor subtly implying that we should retreat to the traditional ways of an earlier time. Even if we wanted to, there is no turning back the clock of social change.

Throughout this book, Mort has suggested actions he believes men and women can take to resolve some of the conflict between the sexes. I would like to end this epilogue with a few suggestions of my own.

Let me begin by saying that I see individual action impeded by the slowness with which our culture and its institutions are responding to change. It is essential that our government, our health and educational organizations, and our industries recognize that people who work outside the home are of both sexes. These institutions must act responsibly toward their employees, men and women, who are part of family systems, and develop forward-looking policies in the areas of:

- Quality child care
- Parental leave (paternity and maternity, sick leave for children and elderly parents)
- Meaningful, legitimate part-time work
- Realistic travel and relocation requirements
- Up-to-date benefit and retirement options.

We must reject lip service to, but applaud any effort toward, acknowledging that family life is valued and

166

important in our society. We need to teach both boys and girls how to succeed in the work world and to be good parents if they so choose. And for goodness sake, let's get an affordable, dependable, *efficient* housekeeping industry developed to relieve us of some of those caretaking activities!

While we are on the subject of caretaking, let us deal with this area. First, I think that it would be useful if women limited the amount of time devoted to it. As we all are aware, these activities can eat up all of our time if we allow them to.

Next, if you are sharing your life with a man, the options available for handling the caretaking aspects of a household are as follows:

1. *You do it all* (probably not an acceptable option to you).

2. *He does it all* (probably not an acceptable option to him).

3. *The two of you share it all* (an option easier said than done, but possible under the special circumstances of having a uniquely open and negotiated relationship).

4. *The two of you hire someone else to do it all* (probably an acceptable option if you have the financial resources, openness of mind, and someone who is willing to find and manage the "someone else").

5. *The two of you share some of the caretaking and hire someone (or someones) to do the rest* (probably the most reasonable option for people who can afford it and whose relationship is good enough to be able to tolerate working out the details).

6. *The two of you get family members to share the caretaking* (including children and even houseguests!).

To get things in real perspective, ask your partner whether, if the two of you split up and to save money he decided to share living quarters with another man, would he expect the other guy to do all of the caretaking that you now do?

Even in good relationships women will need to educate men as to the "what's in it for them" to get them more involved in caretaking.

From all that we have learned about men from Mort and from what we know about how difficult it is for the human animal (male and female) to change, I just don't think men are going to take on new caretaking activities (which would represent, after all, major behavior changes) without their seeing some direct personal benefit.

So let me give you some ammunition for taking the "what's in it for you" case to him. Basically you can tell your man that there are three major benefits, potentially, that he stands to gain from getting more involved with caretaking:

1. more time with you
2. a happier, healthier you; and
3. a better relationship with you.

You can tell him that research has shown that partners, male or female, who are continually overwhelmed with caretaking activities often end up feeling resentful and angry. And over a period of time these built-up feelings can result both in physical and emotional symptoms and in interpersonal conflicts.

Of course, it is in your best interest and his to make sure that he does reap some of the possible benefits of ongoing caretaking that have just been described. At the very least, reward his behavior with a word of appreciation or a thank you. That just makes good sense. Who knows, this might even serve as a model for his future behavior toward you.

If there is one common denominator in the lives of the men and women about whom Mort has written, it is their individual desire for more care. Having care in your life is a lot like having self-esteem — you can never really have too much of it. But at this particular time and in this particular culture, it appears that many are feeling a real deficit. Why?

We have seen how some women are unaware of having become "too busy" to give care or have confused it with caretaking. Perhaps this comes from a growing devaluation of female caregiving behaviors in favor of male-valued ones, such as achieving. Men are not taught to be nurturing. In the male world, "doing" has always been more highly valued than "giving."

I think women have lost sight of how special we are. From our mothers and our grandmothers and those before them, we have inherited the extraordinary gift of caregiving, which throughout humankind has been like a torch that lighted up and nourished the world. With this gift we can do what most men cannot — soothe, and heal, and comfort, and calm, and support, and strengthen. Best of all, we can help people feel appreciated and loved. Is there anything more important than that?

So as of this moment why don't we commit ourselves to taking the time for caregiving in our lives, both to giving and receiving it? Let's pass the torch to our daughters, and to our sons. Why don't we begin teaching the men in our lives how to give it, and let them in on the secret that they'll get back a multiple of whatever they give (especially from the women in their lives)? I think we can be instrumental in changing the theme of today's man from "Adam Was a Lonely Guy" to "Real Men Really Care."

What do we have to lose?

Suggested Readings

Men

Bell, Donald H. *Being A Man: The Paradox of Masculinity*. Brattleboro, VT: Lewis Publishing Co., 1982.

Druck, Ken, and James C. Simmons. *The Secrets Men Keep*. Garden City, NY: Doubleday, 1985.

Emerson, Gloria. *Some American Men*. New York: Simon and Schuster, 1985.

Farrel, Warren. *Why Men Are the Way They Are*. New York: McGraw-Hill, 1986.

Fishel, Elizabeth. *The Men in Our Lives*. New York: William Morrow, 1985.

Friday, Nancy. *Men in Love*. New York: Delacorte Press, 1980.

Garfinkel, Perry. *In a Man's World: Father, Son, Brother, Friend, and Other Roles Men Play*. New York: New American Library, 1985.

Gerzon, Mark. *A Choice of Heroes*. Boston: Houghton Mifflin, 1982.

Gould, Roger L. *Transformations: Growth and Change in Adult Life.* New York: Simon and Schuster, 1978.

Kiley, Dan. *The Peter Pan Syndrome.* New York: Avon Books, 1983.

Levinson, Daniel J. *The Seasons of a Man's Life.* New York: Ballantine Books, 1978.

McGill, Michael E. *The McGill Report on Male Intimacy.* New York: Holt, Rinehart and Winston, 1985.

Naifeh, Steven, and Gregory White Smith. *Why Can't Men Open Up?.* New York: Clarkson N. Potter, 1984.

Nolen, William A. *Crisis Time! Love, Marriage and the Male at Midlife.* New York: Dodd, Mead, 1984.

Pesmen, Curtis. *How a Man Ages.* New York: Esquire Press, 1984.

Pleck, Elizabeth H. and Joseph H. *The American Man.* Englewood Cliffs, NJ: Prentice-Hall, 1980.

Pleck, Joseph H. *The Myth of Masculinity.* Cambridge, MA: The MIT Press, 1982.

Tiger, Lionel. *Men in Groups.* New York: Marion Boyars Publishers, 1984.

Fathers and Child Rearing

Auerbach, Stevanne, and Linda Freedman. *Choosing Child Care.* San Francisco: Parents and Child Care Resources, 1976.

Bayard, Robert T., and Jean Bayard. *Your Acting-Up Teenager.* San Jose, CA: Accord Press, 1981.

Briggs, Dorothy Corkille. *Your Child's Self-Esteem.* New York: Doubleday, 1970.

Cosby, Bill. *Fatherhood.* New York: Dolphin/Doubleday, 1986.

Dunn, Rita, and Kenneth Dunn. *How to Raise Independent and Professionally Successful Daughters.* Englewood Cliffs, NJ: Prentice-Hall, 1977.

Faber, Adele, and Elaine Mazlish. *How to Talk So Kids Will Listen and How to Listen So Kids Will Talk.* New York: Rawson Wate, 1980.

Farson, Richard. *Birthrights.* New York: Penguin Books, 1974.

Ginott, Haim G. *Between Parent and Child.* New York: Avon Books, 1965.

Glickman, Beatrice Marden, and Nesha Bass Springer. *Who Cares for the Baby? Choices in Child Care.* New York: Schocken Books, 1978.

Greenberg, Martin, M.D. *Birth of a Father.* New York: Avon Books, 1985.

Greene, Bob. *Good Morning, Merry Sunshine.* New York: Atheneum, 1984.

Hawes, Gene R., and Helen G. and Martin S. Weiss. *How to Raise Your Child to Be a Winner.* New York: Rawson Wade, 1980.

Levine, James A. *Who Will Raise the Children? New Options for Fathers (and Mothers).* Philadelphia: J. B. Lippincott, 1976.

Pogrebin, Letty Cottin. *Growing Up Free.* New York: McGraw-Hill, 1980.

Wallerstein, Judith S., and Joan Berlin Kelly. *Surviving the Breakup: How Children and Parents Cope with Divorce.* New York: Basic Books, 1980.

Whelan, Elizabeth M. *A Baby? . . . Maybe: A Guide to Making the Most Fateful Decision of Your Life.* New York: Bobbs-Merrill, 1975.

Relationships

Archer, John, and Barbara Lloyd. *Sex and Gender.* New York: Press Syndicate of the University of Cambridge, 1985.

Blumstein, Philip, and Pepper Schwarts. *American Couples*. New York: William Morrow, 1983.

Comfort, Alex, ed. *The Joy of Sex*. New York: Crown, 1972.

Curran, Dolores. *Stress and the Healthy Family*. Minneapolis: Winston Press, 1985.

Fisher, Roger, and William Ury. *Getting to Yes: Negotiating Agreement Without Giving In*. Boston: Houghton Mifflin, 1981.

Lerner, Harriett Goldhor. *The Dance of Anger*. New York: Harper & Row, 1985.

Lipman-Blumen, Jean. *Gender Roles and Power*. Englewood Cliffs, NJ: Prentice-Hall, 1984.

Mornel, Pierre. *Passive Men, Wild Women*. New York: Ballantine Books, 1979.

Pogrebin, Letty Cottin. *Family Politics*. New York: McGraw-Hill, 1983.

Rubin, Lillian B. *Intimate Strangers*. New York: Harper & Row, 1983.

―――. *Just Friends: The Role of Friendship in Our Lives*. New York: Harper & Row, 1985.

Satir, Virginia. *Peoplemaking*. Palo Alto, CA: Science and Behavior Books, 1972.

Seward, John P. and Georgene H. *Sex Differences: Mental and Temperamental*. Lexington, MA: Lexington Books, 1980.

Shaevitz, Marjorie Hansen and Morton H. *Making It Together as a Two-Career Couple*. Boston: Houghton Mifflin, 1980.

Tavris, Carol. *Anger*. New York: Simon and Schuster, 1982.

Tavris, Carol, and Carole Offir. *The Longest War*. New York: Harcourt Brace Jovanovich, 1977.

Weitzman, Lenore J. *The Divorce Revolution: The Unexpected Social and Economic Consequences for Women and Children in America*. New York: The Free Press, 1985.

Whitney, Charlotte. *Win-Win Negotiations for Couples*. Gloucester, MA: Para Research, Inc., 1986.

Women

Bardwick, Judith M. *In Transition*. New York: Holt, Rinehart and Winston, 1979.

Baruch, Grace, Rosalind Barnett, and Caryl Rivers. *Lifeprints*. New York: McGraw-Hill, 1983.

Bernard, Jessie. *The Female World*. New York: Free Press, 1981.

———. *Women, Wives, Mothers*. Chicago: Aldine, 1975.

Blotnick, Srully. *Otherwise Engaged: The Personal Lives of Successful Career Women*. New York: Facts on File Publications, 1985.

Cowan, Connell, and Melvyn Kinder. *Smart Women, Foolish Choices*. New York: Clarkson N. Potter, 1985.

Dowling, Colette. *The Cinderella Complex*. New York: Summit Books, 1981.

Eichenbaum, Luise, and Susie Orbach. *Understanding Women*. New York: Basic Books, 1983.

Friedan, Betty. *The Second Stage*. New York: Summit Books, 1981.

Gilligan, Carol. *In a Different Voice*. Cambridge: Harvard University Press, 1983.

Hennig, Margaret, and Anne Jardim. *The Managerial Woman*. New York: Pocket Books, 1978.

Josefowitz, Natasha. *Paths to Power*. Reading, MA: Addison-Wesley, 1980.

Norwood, Robin. *Women Who Love Too Much*. Los Angeles: Jeremy P. Tarcher, Inc., 1985.

Sargent, Alice G. *Beyond Sex Roles*. St. Paul, MN: West, 1977.

————. *The Androgynous Manager*. New York: AMA-COM, 1983.

Shaevitz, Marjorie Hansen. *The Superwoman Syndrome*. New York: Warner Books, 1984.

Witkin-Lanoil, Georgia. *The Female Stress Syndrome*. New York: Newmarket Press, 1984.